Managing education:
theory and practice

OPEN UNIVERSITY PRESS

Management in Education Series

Editor

Tony Bush

Senior Lecturer in Educational Policy and Management
at The Open University

The series comprises five volumes which cover important topics within the
field of educational management. The articles present examples of theory
and practice in school and college management. The authors discuss many
of the major issues of relevance to educational managers in the post-
Education Reform Act era.

The five readers are components of The Open University M.A. in
Education module *E818 Management in Education*. Further information about
this course and the M.A. programme may be obtained by writing to the
Higher Degrees Office, The Open University, PO Box 49, Walton Hall,
Milton Keynes, MK7 6AD.

TITLES IN THE SERIES

Managing Education: Theory and Practice
Tony Bush (ed.)

Approaches to Curriculum Management
Margaret Preedy (ed.)

Financial Management in Education
Rosalind Levačić (ed.)

Human Resource Management in Education
Colin Riches and Colin Morgan (eds)

Educational Institutions and their Environments:
Managing the Boundaries
Ron Glatter (ed.)

Managing education: theory and practice

EDITED BY
Tony Bush
at The Open University

OPEN UNIVERSITY PRESS
MILTON KEYNES · PHILADELPHIA
in association with The Open University

Open University Press
12 Cofferidge Close
Stony Stratford
Milton Keynes MK11 1BY

and
1900 Frost Road, Suite 101
Bristol, PA 19007, USA

First Published 1989

British Library Cataloguing in Publication Data
Bush, Tony, *1943–*
   Managing education: theory and practice. –
   (Management in education)
   1. Great Britain. Educational institutions.
   Management
   I. Title   II. Series
   371.2'00941

   ISBN 0-335-09243-8
      0-335-09242-X (paper)

Library of Congress Cataloging in Publication Number Available

Typeset by Rowland Phototypesetting Ltd
Bury St Edmunds, Suffolk
Printed in Great Britain by Biddles Ltd
Guildford and King's Lynn

Contents

Acknowledgements

All possible care has been taken to trace ownership of the material included in this volume, and Open University Press would like to make grateful acknowledgement for permission to reproduce it here.

1 T. Bush (1989). Commissioned for this collection.
2 M. Weber (1947). *The Theory of Social and Economic Organization*, Chapter III, Section II, New York, Free Press.
3 P. Harling (ed.) (1984). *New Directions in Educational Leadership*, pp. 7–19, Lewes, Falmer Press.
4 T. Noble and B. Pym (1970). 'Collegial authority and the receding locus of power', *British Journal of Sociology*, Vol. 21, pp. 431–45, London, Routledge.
5 R. J. Campbell (1985). *Developing the Primary School Curriculum*, Chapter 10, pp. 152–68, San Diego, Calif., Holt, Rinehart and Winston, Inc.
6 J. V. Baldridge (1971). *Power and Conflict in the University*, Chapter II, pp. 15–24, reprinted by permission of John Wiley & Sons, Inc., New York, USA.
7 E. Hoyle (1986). *The Politics of School Management*, Chapter 6, pp. 125–49, Sevenoaks, Hodder & Stoughton.
8 T. B. Greenfield (1973). 'Organizations as social interventions', *Journal of Applied Behavioral Science*, Vol. 9, No. 5, pp. 552–74, JAI Press Inc., USA.
9 R. Best, P. Ribbins and C. Jarvis with D. Oddy (1983). *Education and Care*, Chapter 3, pp. 57–81, Oxford, Heinemann Educational Books Limited.
10 Reprinted by permission of Harvard Business School Press, Boston, MA. Excerpts from *Leadership and Ambiguity: The American College*

President, 2nd edn., by Michael D. Cohen and James G. March. Copyright © 1974 by the Carnegie Foundation for the Advancement of Training. Copyright © 1986 by the President and Fellows of Harvard College.

11 K. E. Weick (1976). 'Educational organizations as loosley coupled systems', *Administrative Science Quarterly*, Vol. 21, No. 1, pp. 1–9, 16–19, *Administrative Science Quarterly*, USA.

12 L. Bell (1989). Commissioned for this collection.

13 J. L. Davies and A. W. Morgan (1983). 'Management of higher education institutions in a period of contradiction and uncertainty', *Approaches to Post-School Management* edited by O. Boyd-Barrett, T. Bush, J. Goodey, I. McNay and M. Preedy, pp. 157–88, London, Harper and Row.

I should like to thank Beryl Bush for her help in preparing the manuscript for publication and Helen Knowles for typing successive drafts of Chapter 1.

1

The nature of theory in educational management

Tony Bush

The education service is undergoing a period of radical change. The 1988 Education Reform Act is the most important piece of educational legislation since the Second World War. The Act provides for a National Curriculum and for regular assessment of pupils at 7, 11, 14 and 16 years of age. Schools with more than 200 pupils will have substantially increased responsibilities for finance and staff under the new scheme for the Local Management of Schools. The provision for open enrolment gives schools the opportunity to recruit additional pupils up to their physical capacity. The Act also enables schools to opt out of local education authority control and become Grant-maintained Schools (GMS), financed by the Department of Education and Science (DES).

The Reform Act represents the most important stage in the changing pattern of relationships within the education service. The DES has acquired a whole range of new powers in relation to the curriculum, schemes for financial delegation and the approval of GMS applications. Local education authorities will lose much of their day-to-day control of schools and colleges as powers are devolved to institutions. Schools will have much greater responsibility for the management of staff, pupil admissions and finance, together with the right to seek withdrawal from the local authority system. Within schools there is an enhanced role for the new governing bodies established under the 1986 Education Act.

The new responsibilities imposed on schools and colleges by the 1988 Act will place a premium on the effective management of these institutions. Headteachers, principals and other senior staff will have to perform tasks formerly undertaken by LEA officers. People with training and experience in curriculum and pedagogy will have to acquire new skills in staff management, finance and marketing to lead their schools into the competitive period which will follow the implementation of the Act. School management training has been a national priority since 1983 and will become even more important in the post-Reform Act era.

According to Glatter (1979, p. 16), educational management is concerned with 'the internal operation of educational institutions, and also with their relationships with their environments, that is, the communities in which they are set, and with the governing bodies to which they are formally responsible'. School and college leaders generally play a key role in formulating the aims or goals of the institution. They have a particular responsibility for establishing and maintaining an effective management structure. Heads and principals are important participants in the process of decision making and they have a major role in maintaining good relationships with groups and individuals in the external environment.

The relevance of theory

All these managerial functions might be regarded as essentially practical activities. Setting goals, making decisions and building relationships all involve action. It might be thought that simply repeating these tasks would eventually lead to managerial excellence – 'practice makes perfect'. Certainly, practitioners often stress the relevance of practical experience and the remoteness of theory, as Hughes (1986, pp. 3 and 31) points out:

> Theory and practice are uneasy, uncomfortable bedfellows, particularly when one is attempting to understand the complexities of human behaviour in organisational settings, and still more so if the purpose in seeking to achieve such insight is to influence and improve the practice. . . . It has been customary for practitioners to state the dichotomy in robust terms: airy-fairy theory versus down-to-earth practice.

Some practitioners, then, are dismissive of theories and concepts because they are thought to be remote from the realities of schools and classrooms. If teachers and school and college leaders shun theory then they must rely on their experience as a guide to action. In deciding on the most appropriate response to a particular problem they draw on a range of options suggested by previous encounters with this type of issue. If pressed to explain the reasons for the decision, the practitioner is likely to say that it is simply 'common sense'. However, this is often based on an implicit theory of the best way to deal with the situation. 'Commonsense knowledge . . . inevitably carries with it unspoken assumptions and unrecognized limitations. Theorising is taking place without it being acknowledged as such' (Hughes, 1986, p. 31). Managers who operate on the basis of an unrecognized theory tend to have a unidimensional outlook on organizational life. 'Understanding organisations is nearly impossible when the manager is unconsciously wed to a single, narrow perspective. . . . To be locked into a single path is likely to produce error and self-imprisonment' (Bolman and Deal, 1984, p. 4).

The aim of this book is to make theory explicit and demonstrate its relevance to practical situations in schools and colleges. Landers and Myers (1977, p. 365) dispute the claim that theory has little to offer managers in education: 'There is nothing more practical than a good theory. . . . It can . . . help the practitioner to unify and focus his [*sic*] views on an organisation, on his role and relationships within the organisation, and on the elusive phenomena of leadership and achievement.'

Theory provides a rationale for decision making. It helps managers by giving them a basis for action. Without a frame of reference decisions could become purely arbitrary. It is not enough simply to note the facts of a situation and make a decision based on those facts. All such evidence requires interpretation. Familiarity with the arguments and insights of theorists enables the school or college manager to deploy a range of experience and understanding in resolving problems. An appreciation of theory may also reduce the time required to achieve managerial effectiveness by obviating the need for certain levels of experience. In this sense theory may be regarded as a distillation of the experience of others.

The nature of theory

The acquisition of theory is made more complex by the bewildering range of approaches espoused by the many commentators on education. There is no single all-embracing theory to guide practitioners as they grapple with their problems. This is because theory in educational management comprises a series of perspectives rather than an all-embracing 'scientific' truth. House (1981) explains the nature of educational theory thus:

> Our understanding of knowledge utilization processes is conceived not so much as a set of facts, findings, or generalisations but rather as distinct perspectives which combine facts, values, and presuppositions into a complex screen through which knowledge utilization is seen.
>
> Whichever screen one adopts leads one to focus on certain features of knowledge utilization events, to advocate certain policies rather than others, and to conduct certain types of research and evaluation studies. Through a particular screen one sees certain events, but one may see different scenes through a different screen . . .
>
> These 'paradigms' are not the same as those attributed by Kuhn to physical science. Kuhn (1970) saw scientific fields of endeavour as having a set of beliefs, values, and techniques that are shared within a field of scientific inquiry. Eventually the dominant paradigm is challenged by anomalous facts that cannot be explained by the old

paradigm. A new paradigm emerges which can explain these new facts. However, the physical world itself remains constant.

The action perspectives, by contrast, 'describe' or operate in a social or political world that is itself changing. . . . The perspectives rest more upon a professional consensus of what is possible and relevant and valued rather than upon a scientific consensus as to what is true. . . . The perspective is a 'way of seeing' a problem rather than a rigid set of rules and procedures.

(House, 1981, pp. 17 and 20)

The existence of several different perspectives creates what Bolman and Deal (1984) describe as 'conceptual pluralism'. Each theory has something to offer in explaining behaviour and events in educational institutions. A further complication is that these approaches all tend to be normative, that is they reflect the theorists' beliefs about how organizations *should* be managed. Often these perspectives are advocated so zealously that they tend to cloud rather than illuminate reality:

Students of educational management who turn to organisational theory for guidance in their attempt to understand and manage educational institutions will find not a single, universally-applicable theory but a multiplicity of theoretical approaches each jealously guarded by its particular epistemic community.

(Ribbins, 1986, p. 223)

Several writers on organization and management theory attempt to impose order on the confusing variety of perspectives by presenting them in distinct groups or bundles (Bolman and Deal, 1984; Bush, 1986; Cuthbert, 1984; Ellstrom, 1983; Enderud, 1980; House, 1981; Sergiovanni, 1984). The remaining chapters in this book present or illustrate five major theoretical models or perspectives. These are bureaucratic, collegial, political, subjective and ambiguity models. Some of the articles explain the perspective whereas others illustrate the application of one of the models in a British school or college.

The development of theory

The chronology of theory development in educational management has been well documented (Hughes, 1986). A distinction can be made between organization theory and management theory. The latter has a narrower focus and tends to be more practical. However, the distinction is not clear-cut because management theory is grounded in organization theory which in turn has implications for management practice (Hoyle, 1986).

Frederick Taylor was the influential figure of the scientific management movement which was dominant in the early years of the twentieth century. He regarded workers as essentially rational beings who could be expected to operate like machines to increase productivity. Henri Fayol was another important writer during this period. He defined several principles of management which are still influential in many organizations, including schools and colleges. These include division of labour, authority, unity of command and unity of direction.

The works of Taylor and Fayol were seminal contributions to management theory, whereas the first major writer on organization theory was Max Weber. He defined the essentials of bureaucracy and had a significant influence on the subsequent development of this line of theory. Weber advocated a clear-cut division of labour, a hierarchical authority structure and a system of rules and regulations. These concepts are consistent with the principles of classical management expounded by Taylor, Fayol and their successors. Chapter 2 presents an extract from one of Weber's most important works.

Aspects of Weber's theory are clearly relevant to educational institutions, as Hughes (1986, p. 8) suggests: 'Schools and colleges, particularly if they are large, conform to a considerable degree to Weber's specification of bureaucracy.' However, there are few studies which apply the bureaucratic model to British education. One exception is the piece by Paul Harling which forms Chapter 3 of the present volume. Harling links the main precepts of Weber's theory to English schools.

The pervasive influence of bureaucratic and other rational models on schools and colleges is confirmed by the fact that all the other perspectives tend to be tested against the bureaucratic 'norm'. A major criticism of this approach is that it neglects the individual qualities of people and regards them as part of the organizational structure, slotting into defined positions in the hierarchy. Schools and colleges are staffed mainly by professionals who require substantial discretion in performing their teaching role. The bureaucratic model does not satisfactorily explain the contribution of professional staff to the management of educational institutions.

The vital role of teacher professionals in the management of education is at the heart of collegial or democratic models. These approaches reject the concept of hierarchy and assert that decisions should be based on professional discretion rather than bureaucratic rules and regulations. Policies are assumed to emerge through a process of discussion leading to professional consensus. Hierarchical authority is supplanted by the authority of expertise which is regarded as the hallmark of the professional.

Collegial approaches in British education originated in the Oxford and Cambridge colleges:

> Collegium designates a structure or structures in which members have equal authority to participate in decisions which are binding on each of them. It usually implies that individuals have discretion to perform their main operations in their own way, subject only to minimal collegial controls.
>
> (Becher and Kogan, 1980, p. 67)

The collegial model is particularly evident in the extensive committee system which operates within most universities and polytechnics. Decisions are taken within the complex network of committees instead of remaining the responsibility of the principal or vice-chancellor. Chapter 4 by Noble and Pym outlines this collegial approach and shows the obfuscation which can result as responsibility for decisions is lost in a maze of committees.

The collegial model has been adopted in most universities and in institutions of further and higher education but its application to schools has been more selective. In part this is because of the tradition of all-powerful heads and the bureaucratic assumption that they alone have the responsibility for school management. Collegial approaches constitute a major challenge to the hegemony of headteachers:

> The idealised 'collegial school' has small working groups of teachers feeding back suggestions for school-wide change to the collectivity of the whole staff meeting for decision-making. These working groups are usually led by curriculum 'leaders' or 'consultants' who might also work alongside teacher-colleagues. . . . Collegiality is likely to reduce the predominance of the headteacher.
>
> (Southworth, 1988, pp. 51 and 53)

Collegial theories are at an early stage of development and much of the writing is rather tentative. In the article by Jim Campbell which constitutes Chapter 5 of this volume, the author concedes that the analysis is speculative. However, the discussion is well supported by a historical perspective and by empirical studies of primary school practice.

Collegial models are espoused by many heads and other senior staff in schools and colleges. They are attractive approaches because they acknowledge the skills and knowledge of professionals and advocate the participation of staff in decision making. However, empirical evidence of the existence of collegium, particularly in schools, tends to be sketchy and incomplete. A major weakness of this perspective is the assumption that decisions are reached by consensus. As Baldridge *et al.* (1978, pp. 33–4) point out, the harmony bias of collegial models underestimates the potential for conflict: 'The collegial model . . . fails to deal adequately with the problem of *conflict* . . . [it] neglects the prolonged battles that precede consensus and the fact that the consensus actually represents the prevalence of one group over another.'

The centrality of power and conflict in educational decision making is recognized fully by the political models. These approaches acknowledge the prevalence of group decision making but claim that the process is characterized by conflict. Interest groups jockey for advantage within institutions and there is extensive bargaining and negotiation before the conflict is resolved, usually on the basis of the relative power of the participants. Perhaps the most influential writer on political theories in education is the New York professor J. V. Baldridge, and an extract from his seminal work on the political model is included as Chapter 6 of this volume.

Political models have received considerable attention in Britain and there have been several articles on their application to schools. The British Educational Management and Administration Society (BEMAS) devoted its 1981 conference to 'the politics of educational improvement' and a subsequent volume of the Society's journal was dedicated to micropolitics, a term sometimes preferred by British writers. Eric Hoyle (1986) prepared one of the keynote papers for the BEMAS conference and he subsequently expanded on his ideas in a book entitled *The Politics of School Management*. An extract from this work appears as Chapter 7 in the present volume.

One of the most trenchant critics of bureaucratic models is the Canadian writer Thomas Greenfield. He rejects the concept of the institution as a concrete reality and argues that individuals have a subjective perception of the organization. In this view events have different meanings for the various participants in schools and colleges. Subjective theorists also challenge the primacy of organizational structure, preferring to emphasize process and behaviour. Gray (1982) claims that 'structure cannot be imposed on an organisation, it can only derive from what people do'. Greenfield also dismisses the notion of organizations as goal-seeking entities, arguing that it is individuals who have purposes rather than institutions. Greenfield's ideas are enunciated in the article which forms Chapter 8 of this book.

The belief that there may be many different interpretations of events was tested by an important piece of research in a comprehensive school in a London suburb. Ron Best and his colleagues examined the nature of pastoral care in 'Rivendell', comparing practice with the 'conventional wisdom' of the school as a caring institution. The researchers identify five different perspectives on pastoral care, thus lending some empirical support to the strictures of the subjective theorists. Best *et al.* (1983) reported their research in a book entitled *Education and Care*. An extract from this work is included as Chapter 9 of the present volume.

Another criticism levelled at bureaucratic models is that they assume that organizations are stable and predictable with clear goals. Ambiguity models, by contrast, stress the uncertainty and complexity of institutional life. These ideas are associated with a group of theorists from the USA. One of them describes the jumbled reality in many organizations:

> Theories of choice underestimate the confusion and complexity surrounding actual decision making. Many things are happening at once; technologies are changing and poorly understood; alliances, preferences, and perceptions are changing; problems, solutions, opportunities, ideas, people, and outcomes are mixed together in a way that makes their interpretation uncertain and their connections unclear.
>
> (March, 1982)

The most important of the ambiguity theories is the garbage can model developed by Michael Cohen and James March. These authors claim that educational institutions are characterized by uncertain goals, unclear technology and fluid participation in decision making. They are also subject to changing demands from their environments. An extract from their innovative book, *Leadership and Ambiguity* (1986), is included as Chapter 10 of this volume.

An alternative way of conceptualizing organizational ambiguity is the loose coupling metaphor discussed by Karl Weick. Loose coupling is taken to indicate that coupled events are responsive but that each event retains its own identity. Thus school or college departments may respond to other units within the institution but still preserve their separation from such groups. Weick's article forms Chapter 11 of this book.

Although the ambiguity theories appear to be plausible there is little empirical evidence to support their applicability to British education. One important exception is the research conducted by Les Bell in a comprehensive school in the Midlands. The author demonstrates how events and behaviour in this newly amalgamated school can be characterized as ambiguous. His findings are reported in a specially commissioned article which forms Chapter 12 of this volume.

The five theories discussed in this book are generally regarded as alternative ways of conceptualizing the organization and management of educational institutions. However, a few writers have attempted to integrate some or all of the models into an overarching framework. John Davies and Anthony Morgan suggest that the garbage can, political, collegial and bureaucratic theories should be viewed as sequential stages in the process of decision making. Their analysis, which is based on higher education, appears as Chapter 13.

Applying the theories

All the models discussed in this book serve to enhance our understanding of educational organizations. I have sought also to demonstrate their relevance to British schools and colleges by presenting evidence from research conducted in educational institutions. An appreciation of theory should enable practitioners to consider and select from a range of strategies in approaching and resolving problems. Each of the perspectives presented here offers a matching strategy to assist in the management of schools and colleges.

One well-known typology of approaches is that presented by Chin and Benne (1974). They identify empirical–rational, normative–re-educative and power–coercive strategies as means of achieving change in organizations. These stances match three of the models discussed in this book. If leaders perceive their school or college as a bureaucratic organization, then they are likely to use an empirical–rational approach. Here it is assumed that individuals will adopt the proposed change if it can be justified by rational argument. If they regard the situation as collegial then they may turn to a normative–re-educative strategy. In this case leaders seek to influence the attitudes and values of staff in order to develop their commitment to new patterns of work. Or if they see the event in terms of conflict they may well adopt a power–coercive stance. The assumption here is that leaders will use their greater resources of power to ensure that other staff comply with their plans and directions. The key to a successful outcome is making an accurate assessment of the nature of the problem and matching the strategy to that assessment.

Chin and Benne's approach can be extended to the other perspectives discussed in this book. Leaders may acknowledge the significance of the subjective model by providing scope for the expression of different interpretations of events. In situations of ambiguity heads and principals may eschew direct involvement in decision making and concentrate on structural and personnel matters. They decide *where* issues should be resolved and select staff in tune with their own educational philosophies rather than expounding their own views on how issues should be resolved.

By matching their managerial strategies to these perspectives, leaders demonstrate the relevance of theory to practice. An appreciation of theory enables the practitioner to make a more accurate diagnosis of the problem and fit the response to the situation. Managerial flexibility requires conceptual pluralism and this in turn depends on a real understanding of the range of possible approaches. If this book contributes to such an understanding it will achieve its purpose.

References

Baldridge, J. V., Curtis, D. V., Ecker, G. and Riley, G. L. (1978). *Policy-Making and Effective Leadership*. Jossey Bass, San Francisco.

Becher, T. and Kogan, M. (1980). *Process and Structure in Higher Education*. Gower, Aldershot.

Best, R., Ribbins, P. and Jarvis, C. with Oddy, D. (1983). *Education and Care*. Heinemann, London.

Bolman, L. G. and Deal, T. E. (1984). *Modern Approaches to Understanding and Managing Organisations*. Jossey Bass, San Francisco.

Bush, T. (1986). *Theories of Educational Management*. Harper and Row, London (1988 reprint by Paul Chapman Publishing).

Chin, R. and Benne, K. (1974). 'General strategies for effecting change in human systems'. In Bennis, W., Benne, K. and Chin, R., *Planning of Change*. Holt, Rinehart and Winston, London.

Cohen, M. D. and March, J. G. (1986). *Leadership and Ambiguity – the American College President*. Harvard Business School Press, Boston (first published 1974 by McGraw-Hill, New York).

Cuthbert, R. (1984). *The Management Process*. E324 Management in Post-Compulsory Education, Block 3, Part 2. Open University Press, Milton Keynes.

Ellstrom, P. E. (1983). 'Four faces of educational organisations'. *Higher Education*, **12**, 231–41.

Enderud, H. (1980). 'Administrative leadership in organised anarchies'. *International Journal of Institutional Management in Higher Education*, **4**(3), 235–53.

Glatter, R. (1979). 'Educational policy and management: One field or two?' *Educational Analysis*, **1**(2), 15–24.

Gray, H. L. (1982). 'A perspective on organisation theory'. *In* Gray, H. L. (ed.), *The Management of Educational Institutions*. Falmer Press, Lewes.

House, E. R. (1981). 'Three perspectives on innovation'. *In* Lehming, R. and Kane, M. (eds), *Improving Schools: Using what we Know*. Sage, Beverley Hills, Calif.

Hoyle, E. (1986). *The Politics of School Management*. Hodder and Stoughton, Sevenoaks.

Hughes, M. (1986). 'Theory and practice in educational management'. *In* Hughes, M., Ribbins, P. and Thomas, H. (eds), *Managing Education: The System and the Institution*. Holt, Rinehart and Winston, London.

Kuhn, T. S. (1970). *The Structure of Scientific Revolutions*. University of Chicago Press, Chicago.

Landers, T. J. and Myers, J. G. (1977). *Essentials of School Management*. W. B. Saunders, Philadelphia.

March, J. G. (1982). 'Theories of choice and making decisions'. *Society*, **20**(1).

Ribbins, P. (1986). 'Organisation theory and the study of educational institutions'. *In* Hughes, M., Ribbins, P. and Thomas, H. (eds), *Managing Education: The System and the Institution*. Holt, Rinehart and Winston, London.

Sergiovanni, T. J. (1984). 'Cultural and competing perspectives in administrative theory and practice'. *In* Sergiovanni, T. J. and Corbally, J. E., *Leadership and Organisational Culture*. University of Illinois Press, Chicago.

Southworth, G. (1988). 'Primary headship and collegiality'. *In* Glatter, R., Preedy, M., Riches, C. and Masterton, M. (eds), *Understanding School Management*. Open University Press, Milton Keynes.

2
Legal authority in a bureaucracy

Max Weber

[. . .]

Legal authority: The pure type with employment of a bureaucratic administrative staff

The effectiveness of legal authority rests on the acceptance of the validity of the following mutually interdependent ideas:

1 That any given legal norm may be established by agreement or by imposition, on grounds of expediency or rational values or both, with a claim to obedience at least on the part of the members of the corporate group. This is, however, usually extended to include all persons within the sphere of authority or of power in question – which in the case of territorial bodies is the territorial area – who stand in certain social relationships or carry out forms of social action which in the order governing the corporate group have been declared to be relevant.

2 That every body of law consists essentially in a consistent system of abstract rules which have normally been intentionally established. Furthermore, administration of law is held to consist in the application of these rules to particular cases; the administrative process in the rational pursuit of the interests which are specified in the order governing the corporate group within the limits laid down by legal precepts and following principles which are capable of generalized formulation and are approved in the order governing the group, or at least not disapproved in it.

3 That thus the typical person in authority occupies an 'office'. In the action associated with his status, including the commands he issues to others, he is subject to an impersonal order to which his actions are oriented. This is true not only for persons exercising legal authority who are in the usual sense 'officials', but, for instance, for the elected president of a state.

4 That the person who obeys authority does so, as it is usually stated, only in his capacity as a 'member' of the corporate group and what he obeys is only 'the law'. He may in this connection be the member of an association, of a territorial commune, of a church, or a citizen of a state.

5 In conformity with point 3, it is held that the members of the corporate group, in so far as they obey a person in authority, do not owe this obedience to him as an individual, but to the impersonal order. Hence, it follows that there is an obligation to obedience only within the sphere of the rationally delimited authority which, in terms of the order, has been conferred upon him.

The following may thus be said to be the fundamental categories of rational legal authority:

1 A continuous organization of official functions bound by rules.

2 A specified sphere of competence. This involves (a) a sphere of obligations to perform functions which has been marked off as part of a systematic division of labour; (b) the provision of the incumbent with the necessary authority to carry out these functions; and (c) that the necessary means of compulsion are clearly defined and their use is subject to definite conditions. A unit exercising authority which is organized in this way will be called an 'administrative organ'.

There are administrative organs in this sense in large-scale private organizations, in parties and armies, as well as in the state and the church. An elected president, a cabinet of ministers, or a body of elected representatives also in this sense constitute administrative organs. This is not, however, the place to discuss these concepts. Not every administrative organ is provided with compulsory powers. But this distinction is not important for present purposes.

3 The organization of offices follows the principle of hierarchy; that is, each lower office is under the control and supervision of a higher one. There is a right of appeal and of statement of grievances from the lower to the higher. Hierarchies differ in respect to whether and in what cases complaints can lead to a ruling from an authority at various points higher in the scale, and as to whether changes are imposed from higher up or the responsibility for such changes is left to the lower office, the conduct of which was the subject of complaint.

4 The rules which regulate the conduct of an office may be technical rules or norms. In both cases, if their application is to be fully rational, specialized training is necessary. It is thus normally true that only a person who has demonstrated an adequate technical training is qualified to be a member of the administrative staff of such an organized group, and hence only such persons are eligible for appointment to official positions. The administrative staff of a rational corporate group thus typically consists of 'officials', whether the organization be devoted to political, religious, economic – in particular, capitalistic – or other ends.

5 In the rational type it is a matter of principle that the members of the administrative staff should be completely separated from ownership of the means of production or administration. Officials, employees and workers attached to the administrative staff do not themselves own the non-human means of production and administration. These are rather provided for their use in kind or in money, and the official is obligated to render an accounting of their use. There exists, furthermore, in principle, complete separation of the property belonging to the organization, which is controlled within the sphere of office, and the personal property of the official, which is available for his own private uses. There is a corresponding separation of the place in which official functions are carried out, the 'office' in the sense of premises, from living quarters.

6 In the rational type case, there is also a complete absence of appropriation of his official position by the incumbent. Where 'rights' to an office exist, as in the case of judges, and recently of an increasing proportion of officials and even of workers, they do not normally serve the purpose of appropriation by the official, but of securing the purely objective and independent character of the conduct of the office so that it is oriented only to the relevant norms.

7 Administrative acts, decisions and rules are formulated and recorded in writing, even in cases where oral discussion is the rule or is even mandatory. This applies at least to preliminary discussions and proposals, to final decisions, and to all sorts of orders and rules. The combination of written documents and a continuous organization of official functions constitutes the 'office' which is the central focus of all types of modern corporate action.

8 Legal authority can be exercised in a wide variety of different forms which will be distinguished and discussed later. The following analysis will be deliberately confined for the most part to the aspect of imperative co-ordination in the structure of the administrative staff. It will consist in an analysis in terms of ideal types of officialdom or 'bureaucracy'.

In the above outline no mention has been made of the kind of supreme head appropriate to a system of legal authority. This is a consequence of certain considerations which can only be made entirely understandable at a later stage in the analysis. There are very important types of rational imperative co-ordination which, with respect to the ultimate source of authority, belong to other categories. This is true of the hereditary charismatic type, as illustrated by hereditary monarchy, and of the pure charismatic type of a president chosen by plebiscite. Other cases involve rational elements at important points, but are made up of a combination of bureaucratic and charismatic components, as is true of the cabinet form of government. Still others are subject to the authority of the chief of other corporate groups, whether their character be charismatic or bureaucratic; thus the formal head of a government department under a parliamentary regime may be a minister who occupies his position because of his authority in a party. The type of rational, legal administrative staff is capable of application in all kinds of situations and contexts. It is the most important mechanism for the administration of everyday profane affairs. For in that sphere, the exercise of authority and, more broadly, imperative co-ordination consists precisely in administration.

The purest type of exercise of legal authority is that which employs a bureaucratic administrative staff. Only the supreme chief of the organization occupies his position of authority by virtue of appropriation, of election, or of having been designated for the succession. But even *his* authority consists in a sphere of legal 'competence'. The whole administrative staff under the supreme authority then consists, in the purest type, of individual officials who are appointed and function according to the following criteria:

1 They are personally free and subject to authority only with respect to their impersonal official obligations.
2 They are organized in a clearly defined hierarchy of offices.
3 Each office has a clearly defined sphere of competence in the legal sense.
4 The office is filled by a free contractual relationship. Thus, in principle, there is free selection.
5 Candidates are selected on the basis of technical qualifications. In the most rational case, this is tested by examination or guaranteed by diplomas certifying technical training, or both. They are *appointed*, not elected.
6 They are remunerated by fixed salaries in money, for the most part with a right to pensions. Only under certain circumstances does the employing authority, especially in private organizations, have a right to terminate the appointment, but the official is always free to resign. The salary scale is primarily graded according to rank in the hierarchy; but in addition to this criterion, the responsibility of the position and the requirements of the incumbent's social status may be taken into account.
7 The office is treated as the sole, or at least the primary, occupation of the incumbent.
8 It constitutes a career. There is a system of 'promotion' according to seniority or to achievement, or both. Promotion is dependent on the judgement of superiors.
9 The official works entirely separated from ownership of the means of administration and without appropriation of his position.
10 He is subject to strict and systematic discipline and control in the conduct of the office.

This type of organization is in principle applicable with equal facility to a wide variety of different fields. It may be applied in profit-making business or in charitable organizations, or in any number of other types of private enterprises serving ideal or material ends. It is equally applicable to political and to religious organizations. With varying degrees of approximation to a pure type, its historical existence can be demonstrated in all these fields.

1 For example, this type of bureaucracy is found in private clinics, as well as in endowed hospitals or the hospitals maintained by religious orders. Bureaucratic organization has played a major role in the Catholic Church. It is well illustrated by the administrative role of the priesthood in the modern church, which has expropriated almost all of the old church benefices, which were in former days to a large extent subject to private appropriation. It is also illustrated by the conception of the universal Episcopate, which is thought of as formally constituting a universal legal competence in religious matters. Similarly, the doctrine of Papal infallibility is thought of as in fact involving a universal competence, but only one which functions *ex cathedra* in the sphere of the office, thus implying the typical distinction between the sphere of office and that of the private affairs of the incumbent. The same phenomena are found in the large-scale capitalistic enterprise; and the larger it is, the greater their role. And this is not less true of political parties. [. . .] Finally, the modern army is essentially a bureaucratic organization administered by that peculiar type of military functionary, the 'officer'.

2 Bureaucratic authority is carried out in its purest form where it is most clearly dominated by the principle of appointment. There is no such thing as a hierarchy of elected officials in the same sense as there is a hierarchical organization of appointed officials. In the first place, election makes it impossible to attain a stringency of discipline even approaching that in the appointed type. For it is open to a subordinate official to compete for elective honours on the same terms as his superiors, and his prospects are not dependent on the superior's judgement.

3 Appointment by free contract, which makes free selection possible, is essential to modern bureaucracy. Where there is a hierarchical organization with impersonal spheres of competence, but occupied by unfree officials – like slaves or dependents, who, however, function in a formally bureaucratic manner – the term 'patrimonial bureaucracy' will be used.

4 The role of technical qualifications in bureaucratic organizations is continually increasing. Even an official in a party or a trade union organization is in need of specialized knowledge, though it is usually of an empirical character, developed by experience, rather than by formal training. In the modern state, the only 'offices' for which no technical qualifications are required are those of ministers and presidents. This only goes to prove that they are 'officials' only in a formal sense, and not substantively, as is true of the managing director or president of a large business corporation. There is no question but that the 'position' of the capitalistic entrepreneur is as definitely appropriated as is that of a monarch. Thus at the top of a bureaucratic organization, there is necessarily an element which is at least not purely bureaucratic. The category of bureaucracy is one applying only

to the exercise of control by means of a particular kind of administrative staff.

5 The bureaucratic official normally receives a fixed salary. By contrast, sources of income which are privately appropriated will be called 'benefices'. Bureaucratic salaries are also normally paid in money. Though this is not essential to the concept of bureaucracy, it is the arrangement which best fits the pure type. Payments in kind are apt to have the character of benefices, and the receipt of a benefice normally implies the appropriation of opportunities for earnings and of positions. There are, however, gradual transitions in this field with many intermediate types. Appropriation by virtue of leasing or sale of offices or the pledge of income from office are phenomena foreign to the pure type of bureaucracy. [. . .]

6 The typical 'bureaucratic' official occupies the office as his principal occupation.

7 With respect to the separation of the official from ownership of the means of administration, the situation is essentially the same in the field of public administration and in private bureaucratic organizations, such as the large-scale capitalistic enterprise.

[. . .]

The monocratic type of bureaucratic administration

Experience tends universally to show that the purely bureaucratic type of administrative organization – i.e. the monocratic variety of bureaucracy – is, from a purely technical point of view, capable of attaining the highest degree of efficiency and is in this sense formally the most rational known means of carrying out imperative control over human beings. It is superior to any other form in precision, in stability, in the stringency of its discipline, and in its reliability. It thus makes possible a particularly high degree of calculability of results for the heads of the organization and for those acting in relation to it. It is finally superior both in intensive efficiency and in the scope of its operations, and is formally capable of application to all kinds of administrative tasks.

The development of the modern form of the organization of corporate groups in all fields is nothing less than identical with the development and continual spread of bureaucratic administration. This is true of church and state, of armies, political parties, economic enterprises, organizations to promote all kinds of causes, private associations, clubs, and many others. Its development is, to take the most striking case, the most crucial phenomenon of the modern Western state. However many forms there may be which do not appear to fit this pattern, such as collegial representative bodies, parliamentary committees, soviets, honorary officers, lay judges, and what not, and however much people may complain about the 'evils of bureaucracy', it would be sheer illusion to think for a moment that continuous administrative work can be carried out in any field except by means of officials working in offices. The whole pattern of everyday life is cut to fit this framework. For bureaucratic administration is, other things being equal, always, from a formal, technical point of view, the most rational type. For the needs of mass administration today, it is completely indispensable. The choice is only that between bureaucracy and dilettantism in the field of administration.

The primary source of the superiority of bureaucratic administration lies in the role of technical knowledge which, through the development of modern technology and business methods in the production of goods, has become completely indispensable. In this respect, it makes no difference whether the economic system is organized on a capitalistic or a socialistic basis. Indeed, if in the latter case a comparable level of technical efficiency were to be achieved, it would mean a tremendous increase in the importance of specialized bureaucracy.

When those subject to bureaucratic control seek to escape the influence of the existing bureaucratic apparatus, this is normally possible only by creating an organization of their own which is equally subject to the process of bureaucratization. Similarly, the existing bureaucratic apparatus is driven to continue functioning by the most powerful interests which are material and objective, but also ideal in character. Without it, a society like our own – with a separation of officials, employees and workers from ownership of the means of administration, dependent on discipline and on technical training – could no longer function. The only exception would be those groups, such as the peasantry, who are still in possession of their own means of subsistence. Even in case of revolution by force or of occupation by an enemy, the bureaucratic machinery will normally continue to function just as it has for the previous legal government.

The question is always who controls the existing bureaucratic machinery. And such control is possible only in a very limited degree to persons who are not technical specialists. Generally speaking, the trained permanent official is more likely to get his way in the long run than his nominal superior, the Cabinet minister, who is not a specialist.

Though by no means alone, the capitalistic system has undeniably played a major role in the development of bureaucracy. Indeed, without it capitalistic production could not continue and any rational type of socialism would have simply to take it over and increase its importance. Its development, largely under capitalistic auspices, has created an urgent need for stable, strict, intensive and calculable administration. It is this need which gives bureaucracy a crucial role in our society as the central element in any kind of large-scale administration. Only by reversion in every field – political, religious, economic, etc. – to small-scale organization, would it be possible to any considerable extent to escape its influence. On the one hand, capitalism in its modern stages of development strongly tends to foster the development of bureaucracy, though both capitalism and bureaucracy have arisen from many different historical sources. Conversely, capitalism is the most rational economic basis for bureaucratic administration and enables it to develop in the most rational form, especially because, from a fiscal point of view, it supplies the necessary money resources.

Along with these fiscal conditions of efficient bureaucratic administration, there are certain extremely important conditions in the fields of communication and transportation. The precision of its functioning requires the services of the railway, the telegraph and the telephone, and becomes increasingly dependent on them. A socialistic form of organization would not alter this fact. It would be a question whether in a socialistic system it would be possible to provide conditions for carrying out as stringent bureaucratic organization as has been possible in a capitalistic order. For socialism would, in fact, require a still higher degree of formal bureaucratization than capitalism. If this should prove not to be possible, it would demonstrate the existence of another of those fundamental elements of irrationality in social systems – a conflict between formal and substantive rationality of the sort which sociology so often encounters.

Bureaucratic administration means fundamentally the exercise of control on the basis of knowledge. This is the feature of it which makes it specifically rational. This consists on the one hand in technical knowledge which, by itself, is sufficient to ensure it a position of extraordinary power. But in addition to this, bureaucratic organizations, or the holders of power who make use of them, have the tendency to increase their power still further by the knowledge growing out of experience in the service. For they acquire through the conduct of office a special knowledge of facts and have available a store of documentary material peculiar to themselves. While not peculiar to bureaucratic organizations, the concept of 'official secrets' is certainly typical of them. It stands in relation to technical knowledge in somewhat the same position as commercial secrets do to technological training. It is a product of the striving for power.

Bureaucracy is superior in knowledge, including both technical knowledge and knowledge of the concrete fact within its own sphere of interest, which is usually confined to the interests of a private business – a capitalistic enterprise. The capitalistic entrepreneur is, in our society, the only type who has been able to maintain at least relative immunity from subjection to the control of rational bureaucratic knowledge. All the rest of the population have tended to be organized in large-scale corporate groups which are inevitably subject to bureaucratic control. This is as inevitable as the dominance of precision machinery in the mass production of goods.

The following are the principal more general social consequences of bureaucratic control:

1 The tendency to 'levelling' in the interest of the broadest possible basis of recruitment in terms of technical competence.
2 The tendency to plutocracy growing out of the interest in the greatest possible length of technical training. Today this often lasts up to the age of 30.

3 The dominance of a spirit of formalistic impersonality, *Sine ira et studio*, without hatred or passion, and hence without affection or enthusiasm. The dominant norms are concepts of straightforward duty without regard to personal considerations. Everyone is subject to formal equality of treatment, i.e. everyone in the same empirical situation. This is the spirit in which the ideal official conducts his office.

The development of bureaucracy greatly favours the levelling of social classes and this can be shown historically to be the normal tendency. Conversely, every process of social levelling creates a favourable situation for the development of bureaucracy; for it tends to eliminate class privileges, which include the appropriation of means of administration and the appropriation of authority as well as the occupation of offices on an honorary basis or as an avocation by virtue of wealth. This combination everywhere inevitably foreshadows the development of mass democracy. [. . .]

The 'spirit' of rational bureaucracy has normally the following general characteristics:

1 Formalism, which is promoted by all the interests which are concerned with the security of their own personal situation, whatever this may consist in. Otherwise the door would be open to arbitrariness and hence formalism is the line of least resistance.

2 There is another tendency, which is apparently in contradiction to the above, a contradiction which is in part genuine. It is the tendency of officials to treat their official function from what is substantively a utilitarian point of view in the interest of the welfare of those under their authority. But this utilitarian tendency is generally expressed in the enactment of corresponding regulatory measures which themselves have a formal character and tend to be treated in a formalistic spirit. This tendency to substantive rationality is supported by all those subject to authority who are not included in the class mentioned above as interested in the security of advantages already controlled. The problems which open up at this point belong in the theory of 'democracy'.

[. . .]

3

The organizational framework for educational leadership

Paul Harling

The educational organization

The educational system in England and Wales can be regarded as a 'complex social organization' (Katz, 1964).[1]* It is 'complex' because it includes many different persons who interact in their performance of many different functions. It is 'social' because 'the participants are interdependent and their actions are socially promulgated and enforced' (Katz, 1964).[2] This emphasis on people and their influence on other people is echoed by Kelly who writes that 'the most important thing to know about organizations is that they do not exist – except in people's minds' (Kelly, 1974),[3] and by Etzioni who refers to organizations as 'social units that pursue specific goals which they are structured to serve' (Etzioni, 1964).[4] At risk of being pedantic it is therefore clear that the educational system as a whole is 'an organization' and that it possesses constituent 'organizations' at various levels. All the participants are thus part of the same organization – although at times the behaviour of some sectors would seem to suggest otherwise.

The distinctive characteristic of an organization is therefore that it has been formally established for the explicit purpose of achieving certain goals. Every organization has a formally instituted pattern of authority and an official body of rules and procedures which are intended to aid the achievement of those goals. However, alongside this formal aspect of the organization are networks of informal relationships and unofficial norms which arise from the interaction of individuals and groups working within the formal structure. Every 'leader' has to be aware of both these aspects as it is their interaction which determines the level and nature of his autonomy and therefore his ability to lead other participants and influence the system as a

*Superscript numerals refer to numbered notes at the end of this chapter.

whole. The importance of considering such theoretical viewpoints is emphasized by Sergiovanni and Starratt when they refer to the various theories of administration, management and leadership as 'alternative windows through which the educational practitioner can view [educational] problems and issues'.[5] They point out that the practitioner is the one qualified to 'build prescription from theory . . . in view of the uniqueness and complexity of the circumstances he faces'.[6] [. . .]

The bureaucratic model

The most widely recognized framework for understanding formal administrative and supervisory structures is the bureaucratic model first articulated methodically by Max Weber. Contrary to the popular view of a bureaucracy being characterized by layers of inefficient functionaries, Weber sees bureaucracy as a form of organization which strives continuously for maximum efficiency through rationally defined structures and processes. Indeed, he believes that 'the decisive reason for the advance of bureaucratic organization has always been its purely technical superiority over other forms of organization'.[7]

Abbott (1965),[8] among others, has outlined Weber's model of ideal bureaucracy, noting how its features are present to some degree in most organizations, including schools and educational systems and sub-systems. It is worth considering these briefly in turn to ascertain the extent of their presence and effect on educational leadership, decision making and organization.

First, organizational tasks are distributed among the various positions as official duties. This implies a division of labour and a degree of specialization enabling the organization to employ personnel on the basis of specific skills and experience. The DES is divided into branches, LEAs are divided into administrative districts and by type of educational institution. Similarly, schools are divided into types, departments are established within schools and there is a clear distinction, except in the case of headteachers, between the administration function and the teaching function.

Secondly, in the classical Weberian model, the positions and offices are organized into a hierarchical authority structure, usually a pyramid. Thus the DES and Parliament have powers of control over LEAs who in turn 'lead' school governors who 'lead' headteachers who 'lead' classroom teachers.

Thirdly, there is a formally established system of rules and regulations governing official decisions and actions. The regulations ensure a degree of uniformity of operation and together with the authority structure make possible the co-ordination of the various activities. Such regulations provide a degree of continuity regardless of changes in personnel, thus promoting stability. In fact there is considerable standardization of textbooks, syllabi, examinations and the like to provide for orderly behaviour, and each LEA has a sytem of issuing bulletins and memoranda on matters of safety, health and the legal rights and obligations of teachers.

Fourthly, officials are expected to assume an impersonal orientation in their contact with 'clients' and other officials. Such detachment is designed to prevent the personal feelings of officials from distorting their rational judgement in carrying out their duties. In schools and LEAs, authority has been generally established on the basis of rational considerations rather than charismatic qualities, participants are expected to apply rules with strict impartiality and thus, by operating in a spirit of 'formalistic impersonality', the typical school system and school has succeeded, to a large extent, in separating organizational rights and obligations from the private lives of individuals.

Fifthly, employment by the organization constitutes a career for participants based on expertise and qualifications. Officers and teachers are appointed by 'normal' competitive procedures and 'career advancements are according to seniority or to achievement or both' (Blau and Scott, 1962).[9] Such features are easily recognized as fundamental to the conditions of employment in the educational organization and encourage the development of 'fair' styles of leadership.

The Weberian model therefore projects an image of certain 'leaders' deliberately controlling the educational system or sub-system by adjusting the 'levers of authority' (Hanson, 1976–7).[10] [. . .] To some degree the educational system is a unique type of organization and, as Parsons[11] and Gouldner,[12] among others, have stressed, Weber's approach fails to recognize the effects of the presence of personnel with 'professional' tendencies and orientations on the process of leadership and decision making in education. The distinction appears to be one of differentiating between the existence of the educational system as an entity in its own right and the 'life' and 'action' which are brought in by the human participants. This distinction is highlighted in the model of administrative and supervisory behaviour which discusses schools in terms of social systems analysis and which was developed by Getzels and Guba.[13]

The social systems model

The constituent organizations of our educational system individually and collectively respond to stimuli from their social environment, and also affect the environment with their 'output'. Getzels and Guba suggest that the context and process of management, of which leadership is a part, can be examined from structural, functional and operational perspectives. Structurally, management and leadership consist of a series of superordinate–subordinate relationships within the system. Functionally, this hierarchy of relationships is the basis for allocating and integrating roles, personnel and facilities on behalf of the goals of the system. Operationally, the management process occurs totally through interpersonal relationships. The emphasis is therefore on people and on the resulting uniqueness of each organization as the participants bring into it needs, interests, expectations and attitudes.

The manager/leader must therefore be aware of, and work within, two dimensions. First, he is concerned with the nomothetic dimension representing the ongoing structure of education which exists and persists regardless of the particular staff employed at a particular time. The structure is defined in terms of roles, such as Secretary of State, Chief Education Officer, Headteacher or Teacher. The roles are defined in terms of the expectations, of the incumbent and others, which are associated with the roles and from which he as the 'leader' will develop his actions. This dimension conveys a model for our educational system as a relatively stable pattern of roles, within which incumbents conform to the expectations attached to them.

However, such a dimension takes no account of the differences between people, and hence is balanced by the idiographic or personal dimension. In this dimension the individual has personally determined goals which are expressed through unique personalities according to unique needs. The idiographic dimension thus represents the idiosyncratic aspect of an organization, which is a function of differences between people. The fundamental concern for a consideration of leadership is therefore whether the educational system uses people to accomplish organizational ends or whether people use the educational system to accomplish human ends.

This model therefore highlights the major dilemma facing someone who wishes to lead. Because the educational system is a human organization the task must be based on both the nomothetic and idiographic dimensions. Leaders are concerned not only with survival and maintenance of the school system, but also with the appropriateness of educational goals, the welfare and development of staff, and with the intellectual, social and emotional development of the 'clients' – the children and students who use and benefit from educational provisions. The dilemma is a recurrent theme of this book but it seems probable that with clear human concerns the system is required to serve its participants and clients, rather than the suggested bureaucratic way which requires individuals, to a large extent, to serve the system.

Consideration of the scope and intensity of the autonomy of leaders and decision makers must depend partly on the nature of this 'organization versus individual' dilemma and whether indeed such a dilemma exists at all. Its persistence as a theme of management and leadership discussions therefore requires some consideration of authority systems in education, with particular emphasis on the authority and power of those participants who find themselves in the role of 'leader'.

Authority systems in education

It has already been suggested that Weber's bureaucratic model of organizational structure and implied behaviour is fundamental. Similarly, Weber's formulation of authority types provides a background for discussion of any participant's organizational authority, power and leadership.

Weber distinguishes three kinds of authority on the basis of their acceptance as a common feature for a particular group within the educational system.[14] Given that 'power' refers to the ability to control the actions of others, 'legitimation' refers to social approval and 'authority' refers to legitimized power, Weber distinguishes three major types of authority and therefore sources of legitimation: legal/rational, charismatic/affective and tradition.[15]

Legal/rational legitimation rests on the acceptance of the supremacy of law and social norms, and compliance is the result of the application of impersonal principles and rules. It is this form of authority which provides a basis for the ideal bureaucratic organization and is particularly applicable to the situation of the Secretary of State and parliament in relation to the educational system as a whole. In a similar way heads of maintained schools are bound by articles of government which set broad limits on their autonomy. Draft articles were set down in a central government White Paper[16] and virtually all LEAs obeyed the advice almost to the last comma.

Therefore, any challenge to the authority of the headteacher to 'lead' his school, perhaps by the staff of the school or 'outsiders', may be countered by reference to the legal establishment of that authority. In addition, headteachers, for example, 'may draw legal legitimation from the many circulars, reports and recommendations which come to them from the local authority administration, the inspectorate, the Department of Education and Science, and from the various consultative committees of the Department' (King, 1973).[17] Some of these are demands, others advisory. King adds to this by pointing out that 'a rational belief in the value of an action can be an important source of legitimation for that action, without an accompanying legal or official codification'.[18] It is therefore a subtle but powerful tool of the leader in the educational system.

Charismatic or affective legitimation rests on a profession of faith in the correctness of a course of action, although that action may not be rationally justifiable to a majority of interested parties. [. . .] The headteacher can decide upon any rules or codes of discipline for his school, with official (i.e. LEA and legal) support, but if his affective legitimation is faulty he will meet significant opposition from his employers, the parents, and possibly the children. To reinforce the previous emphasis on the educational system being a human organization, effective leadership requires the development of both charismatic/affective and legal/rational legitimation.

Traditional legitimation of the educational leaders' authority derives largely from historical beliefs about the role of leaders, and is sometimes based upon outdated practices. There are still some people who believe that leaders at all levels 'know best' what is good for the rest. [. . .] Schools which have encouraged the development of [. . .] parents' associations have found that traditional views, merely because they are based on tradition, are quickly challenged by people of equal or greater intelligence than the proponent of the views. [. . .]

The developing professionalism (including relevant knowledge, skills and attitudes) of teachers and administrators at all levels has produced a fourth source of organizational authority based on professional norms and skills. It is a suitable tool for consideration of the 'organization versus individual' dilemma, mentioned earlier, which bedevils leaders in the educational system. It is particularly noticeable that in schools 'organizational norms and rules often conflict with educo-professional norms'.[19]

The work of Peabody[20] is of great value when, in summarizing the work of Weber, Simon, Bennis and Presthus,[21] he identifies four broad categories of authority: authority of legitimacy, authority of position (including the sanctions which may be part of a leadership decision), authority of competence (including professional skills and experience), and authority of person (including human relations skills). Peabody notes that teachers seemed to value authority of competence higher than authority of person, position or legitimacy, and that authority of position and person were next in importance. In other words, the professional orientation of subordinates is a potent force for a leader, and he needs to recognize and utilize the fact that professionalism exists if he wishes to have an effective base of authority on which to build his decision making and leadership.

The indications would seem to be, therefore, that in general, leaders in the educational system are finding that their bases of authority are changing. The popular view of the leader as one who possesses legal rights, with powers by virtue of his position to impose sanctions and rewards, is being upstaged by his need to display superior competence and possess those leadership qualities as an individual which encourage his views to be adopted. [. . .]

Professional tendencies in education

It seems very likely, in view of the foregoing discussion, that a purely formal model of organizational structure, control and leadership in our educational system would not be useful for any more than a very simplistic analysis of the actual processes of decision making. As Lortie points out with reference to the schools sector:

> the bureaucratic model, in emphasising the formal distribution of authority, does not prepare us for many of the events that actually occur in public schools. Teachers, for example, lay claim to and get, informally, certain types of authority despite lack of formal support for it either in law or in school system constitutions.[22]

Bidwell, in his classic analysis of the school as a formal organization, stresses that we have limited knowledge about the 'interplay of bureaucratization and professionalism in the schools'.[23] This is also true among schools, school governors and LEAs. Hanson adds that the interplay issue is quite significant in understanding questions of educational leadership and decision making 'because teachers as professionals claim allegiance to a set of normative principles representative of the profession as well as to a specialised colleague group'.[24] On the other hand, local education authority officers, and to some extent headteachers, 'must be loyal to the organization that employs them'. In this instance Lortie writes, 'the several strands of hierarchical control, collegial control and autonomy become tangled and complex'.[25] Clearly, to refer to the school and educational system as a *complex* organization is no exaggeration.

[. . .]

Notes

1 Katz, F. E. (1964). 'The school as a complex social organization'. *Harvard Educational Review*, **34**(3).
2 Ibid., p. 428.
3 Kelly, J. (1974). *Organizational Behaviour*. New York, Irwin, p. 1.
4 Etzioni, A. (1964). *Modern Organizations*. Englewood Cliffs, N.J., Prentice-Hall, p. 4.
5 Sergiovanni, T. J. and Starratt, R. J. (1971). *Emerging Patterns of Supervision: Human Perspectives*, New York, McGraw Hill, p. 31.
6 Ibid., p. 31.
7 Gerth, H. and Wright Mills, C. (1947). *From Max Weber; Essays in Sociology*. London, Routledge and Kegan Paul, p. 214.
8 Abbott, M. G. and Lovell, J. T. (eds) (1965). *Change Perspectives in Educational Administration*. Auburn, Auburn University Press.
9 Blau, P. M. and Scott, W. R. (1962). *Formal Organizations: A Comparative Approach*. San Francisco, Chandler, pp. 32–3.
10 Hanson, M. (1976–7). 'Beyond the bureaucratic model: A study of power and autonomy in educational decision making'. *Interchange*, **7**(2), 28.
11 Parsons, T., Introduction, in Weber, M. (1947). *The Theory of Social and Economic Organization*. Translated by Henderson, A. M. and Parsons, T. Glencoe, Free Press, pp. 58–60.
12 Gouldner, A. (1954). *Patterns of Industrial Democracy*. London, Routledge and Kegan Paul, pp. 22–4.
13 Getzels, J. W. and Guba, E. G. (1957). 'Social behaviour and the administrative process'. *School Review*, **65**, 423–41.
14 Henderson and Parsons (1947), *op. cit.*
15 Gerth and Wright Mills (1947), *op. cit.*, p. 9.
16 *Principles of Government in Maintained Secondary Schools* (1944). London, HMSO.
17 King, R. (1973). 'The head teacher and his authority'. In Fowler, G. *et al.* (eds), *Decision Making in British Education*. London, Heinemann, p. 425.
18 Ibid.
19 Sergiovanni and Starratt (1971), *op. cit.*, p. 39.
20 Peabody, R. L. (1962). 'Perceptions of organizational authority: A comparative analysis'. *Administrative Science Quarterly*, **6**(4).

21 Weber, M., in Henderson and Parsons (1947), *op. cit.*; Urwick, L. (1944). *The Elements of Administration*. London, Heinemann; Simon, H. A. *et al.* (1950). *Public Administration*. New York, Macmillan; Bennis, W. G. (1959). 'Leadership theory and administrative behaviour; the problem of authority'. *Administrative Science Quarterly*, **4**; Presthus, R. V. (1960). 'Authority in organizations'. *Public Administration Review*, **20**.

22 Lortie, D. C. (1964). 'The teacher and team teaching; suggestions for long term research'. *In* Shaplin, J. T. and Olds, H. F. (eds), *Team Teaching*. New York, Harper and Row, p. 273.

23 Bidwell, C. (1965). 'The school as a formal organization'. *In* March, J. G., *Handbook of Organizations*. Chicago, Rand McNally, p. 992.

24 Hanson (1976–7), *op. cit.*, p. 27.

25 Lortie (1964), *op. cit.*, p. 1.

[. . .]

4

Collegial authority and the receding locus of power*

Trevor Noble and Bridget Pym

It is evident that the type of authority structure which develops within an organization depends on a number of factors including the location of ownership,[1]† market position,[2] size[3] and the mode of technology employed.[4] These factors have been shown to moderate the extent to which a rational administrative authority emerges, but the rational ethic is itself a prime variable in the context of which all the other determinants operate. Commentators from Weber onwards[5] have emphasized the significance in Western culture of this ethic and of the bureaucratic administrative system which derives from it.

In his celebrated discussion of bureaucracy,[6] Weber of course was not concerned to develop an empirical description of bureaucratic forms responding to the exigencies of empirical reality, but only with the purely formal characteristics of the most rational type of administration. As Mannheim pointed out long ago, however, definitions of rationality may vary according to one's point of view, so that what may be rational in terms of the administration of a large organization may be inconsistent with rationality from the standpoint of the individual worker.[7] Even at the level of the organization, rationality can only be determined with reference to specific goals. Where the goals of an organization are diverse or unclear, or where there is disagreement about them, it will be doubly difficult to determine what would be the most rational system of organization. In Weber's ideal typical bureaucracy, rationality is identified with the apparently

*We would like to acknowledge the encouragement and helpful comments made on earlier drafts of this paper by Dr D. J. Lee of the University of Essex, Professor Lupton of the Manchester Business School and Professor S. B. N. Shimmin of the University of Lancaster.
†Superscript numerals refer to numbered notes at the end of this chapter.

unambiguous goals of the administration, and the limits of competence of each office are strictly defined and ordered hierarchically, each higher office co-ordinating, supervising and authorizing the activities of its immediate inferiors.

In practice one factor which seems particularly alien to the development of this pattern is that of professionalism. Indeed, one of the defining characteristics of the professional is his avowal of a code of practice which commits him to the independent exercise of his own trained judgement.

Dalton has described the conflict of interests between the management and staff 'experts',[8] and Crozier has argued that technical expertise represents a power base from which the experts, 'those who can control the remaining areas of uncertainty', can resist the bureaucratic hierarchy.[9] Similarly, Janowitz argued that technical expertise weakens hierarchical authority,[10] and Blau and Scott have not only questioned the assumption that a hierarchy of authority is essential for co-ordination in complex organizations but also argue that the presence of large bodies of 'professionals' undermines the possibility of a rigid hierarchy of control.[11] The professional, it is said, is employed in the performance of tasks which are not routinizable. He is not therefore easily accommodated within a formalized hierarchy, both because the situations with which he is dealing are non-standard and in addition he may perhaps be expected to be committed to his code of professional practice more strongly than to the goals of the organization which employs him.[12]

The professional's claim of autonomy in the exercise of his professional skills has become the basis for his general social status inside and outside the work situation and this, once established, reinforces his claim for professional respect and the right to be consulted in a wide range of matters which affect both his work and his status. Where such staff form a large proportion of the personnel their effect on the authority structure of an organization is likely to be substantial. Where they dominate the organization we are led to infer that a bureaucratic hierarchy of authority would be very difficult to establish or maintain. An authority structure much closer to what Weber described as 'collegiality' is probable.

In the context of the increasing professionalization of many occupations and the proportionate increase of staff as opposed to line positions, in all sectors of the economy, particularly the tertiary sector,[13] it might be expected that bureaucracy would be in retreat. On the one hand, then, we have the kind of argument exemplified by Blau and Scott which emphasizes the antithesis between the principle of hierarchical authority and the exercise of his professional discretion on the part of the expert.

On the other hand, Michels,[14] though primarily concerned with the location of power within political parties, has argued that the concentration of power and the emergence of an hierarchical pyramid of control is inevitable:

> As organization develops, not only do the tasks of the administration become more difficult and complicated, but further, its duties become

> enlarged and specialized to such a degree that it is no longer possible to take them all in at a single glance. . . . The members have to give up the idea of themselves conducting, or even supervising the whole administration and are compelled to hand these tasks to trustworthy persons.[15]

As a consequence, Michels argues, power is ultimately drawn away from the rank and file membership and a 'rigorously defined and hierarchical bureaucracy emerges'.

Weber himself considered that in the modern world bureaucracy was increasingly likely to supplant other forms of administration:

> For bureaucratic administration is, other things being equal, always, from a formal, technical point of view, the most rational type. For the needs of mass administration today, it is completely indispensable. The choice is only that between bureaucracy and dilettantism in the field of administration.[16]

He argued in particular, though again it is true in the context of political administration, that collegial bodies were rapidly decreasing in importance to be replaced by more clearly defined structures of authority: 'The decisive factor in this development has been the need for rapid, clear decisions, free of the necessity of compromise between different opinions and also free of shifting majorities.'[17]

Collegiality and the hierarchy of committees

Participant observation by the authors in a large service or tertiary organization in the public sector has led us to the view that, though there is something in both points of view, the facts are as usual much more complicated than either allow. The overwhelming majority of staff in the organization in question were professionally qualified. Furthermore, it was clear that the claim inherent in professionalism to self-determination in the exercise of professional functions was extended beyond the areas of strictly professional competence into the sphere of general organizational planning and its detailed execution. The extension of the dominant professional ethic to the administration of a large organization implied the right of status equals to be respected and consulted. This form of authority structure in which legitimate power is vested in a collectivity of equals closely corresponded to that described by Weber as collegiality. Our observations, therefore, were primarily aimed to assess the strength and stability of the collegial authority structure on the one hand or the tendency towards oligarchy on the other.

The organization was divided primarily into specialist departments with semi-autonomous professionally qualified managers and staff of professionally qualified workers.[18] These departments dealt directly with the organizations' clients. Frequently at this level a committee and even sub-committees existed discussing cases and assisting with the departmental administration. Parallel to these specialist or professional departments there were a number of general internal service departments dealing with administrative and financial matters for the organization as a whole, including salaries, centralized records and internal communications and physical services, maintenance, etc.

Superimposed on this base was a complex of co-ordinating committees organized in a federal hierarchy. At a secondary level, groups of specialist departments were represented on a series of committees which in theory integrated the work of departments in related fields or dealing with the same clients. In practice, these secondary interdepartmental committees, though not interfering in the day-to-day work of the specialist departments, were influential in allocating resources between them, regulating workloads, and discussing and submitting for higher approval the operating rules which shape the specialist departments' general schedules of work. While these interdepartmental committees, however, in this way handled a great deal of administration, they submitted their decisions as recommendations to a tertiary or general management committee. This general management committee was a large body totalling 96 members – including all the specialist departmental managers, representatives of their staff and the heads of the general service departments together with a full-time executive chairman. The general management committee in practice rarely discussed policy decisions at any length. Feelings were expressed, forms of words amended, and votes (usually assenting) on sub-committee reports taken. The committee itself could do no more. It was too big and its agendas too cumbersome and generally decisions on policy were dealt with through a series of sub-committees.

Above the general management committee were two fiduciary bodies to whom it was responsible in ways analogous to the responsibility of management in the private sector through a board of directors to the general meeting of shareholders. It was at this level that the source of legitimate authority rested. At the top was a very large corporate body composed of all the members of the general management committee, a similar number of other members of the professional staff and a very large number of representatives of public authorities, related organizations and a number of distinguished or influential individuals drawn mainly from the general field of the organization's external operations. This body had the responsibility of representing the public interest in the activities of the organization and was officially defined in the organization's charter as having absolute power within the organization. Its meetings were entirely formal and rarely did a third of its almost 700 members attend.

Between this representative body and the general management committee an executive board operated in a way analogous to a board of directors in the private sector. Of the 55 members of this board, 24 were professional staff of the organization. The executive board concerned itself primarily with ₕ-term financial planning with the advice of a number of joint sub-committees established between itself and the general management committee. It also was legally empowered to enter into contracts, including contracts of employment, on behalf of the organization. Although legally empowered with the right to do so, this executive board intervened in no noticeable way in the day-to-day or year-to-year conduct of the organization's professional service, apparently invariably accepting recommendations relating to appointments, etc., submitted to it from the general management committee. It was, in fact, our experience that its activities, powers and indeed its very existence remained obscure or unknown as far as the majority of the organization's professional staff were concerned.[19]

In the conclusion to this outline of the five major strata of management and the various minor sub-strata a number of points must be emphasized:

1 First, we must underline the extent of the professional staff's participation in the management of the organization. They played a large part even on the fiduciary board, and committees at the departmental, interdepartmental and general management committee level were staffed overwhelmingly by members of professional status.
2 The same set of individuals served on committees, though not necessarily sub-committees, on at least three levels in the hierarchy. All departmental managers, all of them professionals, served on committees on at least four levels.
3 This pattern of participation was sustained by a generally shared commitment to the value of self-government, and an ideology of organizational autonomy.
4 The management of the organization at all levels (with the possible exception of the primary level departments but frequently even there) was carried out not by individuals but by committees.

This last point is a particularly important one. To a very large extent outside privately owned industry and to a considerable extent within it,[20] decision making occurs within committees. We believe that management theorists neglect this fact to a very considerable extent. Discussions of management almost universally sustain the romantic 'rounding Cape Horn' myth of the master manager making his lonely decisions and alone taking the responsibility if the enterprise should founder. The organization we studied did not correspond to this view. Though the committees of professionals in their secondary administrative role were generally supported by the secretariat of full-time officials from the general service departments, there was no evidence that power had been wholly transferred to these officials.

The most striking feature of the organization to the newcomer or outsider seeking some response from it is the *receding locus of power*. In complex organizations in the spheres of education, industry, administration or commerce, this Kafkaesque experience is very common; wherever or at whatever level one applies to the organization, the 'real' decisions always seem to be taken somewhere else. The lower level officials or committees argue that they, of course, can only make recommendations. Departments must seek the approval of interdepartmental committees, and these in turn can only submit reports and recommendations to the general management committee. It is there we were told that decisions must be made.

At the higher level one finds a different situation. At the very top, the fiduciary board was a formal 'rubber stamp'; at the level of the executive board decisions were of a very general and very long run nature and a policy of non-interference in the details of management was adhered to. In the general management committee, however, though votes are taken and decisions formally reached there was a widespread feeling, frequently expressed even by some of its senior members, of powerlessness, a feeling that decisions were really taken elsewhere. A suggestion that decisions might have been made privately and informally would have been generally resented but nevertheless members of this committee would commonly assure an inquirer that as a committee they could only assent to decisions which had been put up to them from one of the lower-tier committees or a sub-committee. Discussion in fact was effectively delegated to specializing sub-committees who came to grips with the complexities of decision making and were able to formulate recommendations after detailed consideration of alternatives. The superior committee was not equipped to question these in detail.[21]

The common attribution of effective decision making to a higher or lower committee has led the authors to describe the decision-making structure in this organization as an involuted hierarchy. As Weber said, collegiality '. . . divides personal responsibility, indeed in the larger bodies this disappears almost entirely'.[22]

Decision making in the involuted hierarchy

Decision making in the involuted hierarchy of committees was in the hands of committees whose members were conscious of their professional commitment to rational judgement and did not consist of mere crude trials of strength between opposing points of view. No decision was ever all of a piece – each had many facets and endless repercussions. As we have indicated, the process of examining these implications was usually delegated to sub-committees. Frequently, in our experience, however, the terms of reference of a sub-committee were vague. The matters which one committee was discussing were generally contingent on the operations of some other, though this might only emerge after both had been at work for some time.[23]

Thus decision making was not merely a technical matter, a matter of considering expert advice, weighing alternatives, calculating costs and benefits and striking a balance,[24] but of finding room to pursue a project hemmed in by decisions already taken elsewhere, not always with adequate consideration, or by others yet to be taken, or avoiding probable stumbling blocks, and even of neutralizing potential competitors seeking to influence or take the decision themselves.[25]

We have so far considered the system of decision making in the organization only at two superficial levels: first, the formal or overt authority structure of committees and, secondly, the involuted hierarchy which this masks. This in turn contains a still less formal structure of intercursive power relations.[26] We do not suggest that this emergent power structure develops necessarily in response to the 'needs' of the organization, though it certainly seems that without it the involuted hierarchy of committees might well stagnate.[27] Effective decision making in the organization depended on a committee being able to restrict the choices open to other higher- or lower-tier committees in their decision making.[28]

The committees able to achieve this were those who were able to intervene in the process of policy making midway between the initiation of an idea or plan and the engineering of assent at the level of the general management committee or beyond. These larger committees were mainly concerned with the legitimation of decisions effectively already taken and secondarily were sometimes the place 'to let off steam while the kettle is boiled elsewhere'. The powerful 'vetting committees', however, were the place where alternatives which might originate there or in other committees were compared and where opposition to proposals could be effective.

Differentiation of power between committees confers unequal power on the members of the collegial body. Those professionals who achieved membership of committees which were established with the responsibility of vetting the recommendations of other committees or which had been able to acquire this responsibility, clearly had a resource which was not available to their fellow professionals. On the other hand, it was apparent that membership of these powerful committees was not necessarily equally available to all of those who ostensibly enjoyed formal equality of status.

Members of the general management committee were generally selected for the various sub-committees by nomination or, in cases generally considered to be particularly important, by election. For these committees especially, there were sometimes conventional limits to length of service. Nevertheless, some dozen names seemed to recur very frequently among their membership.

The bases of power differentiation

Two interacting processes of differentiation can thus be distinguished. Some sub-committees become more influential than others partly because of their function but also partly because they are composed of powerful men. But one of the main sources of personal influence in a community of status equals is membership of an influential committee. Besides considering the bases of committee power then, we should reconsider the degree of equality among the individual members of the collegial body. Almost all were of formally equal status – departmental manager. Even the non-managerial staff were accorded considerable esteem as fellow professionals and for the most part were encouraged to take an interest in decision making as far as the conventions of the organization would allow. Restricting our considerations to the departmental managers, however, inequalities of esteem became apparent when we examined what Homans referred to as the 'internal' system. Some individuals had achieved popularity or respect, others had not or perhaps had not sought it.

Without postulating any particular psychological theory we can make the assumption that in most organizations there will either be individuals who will seek power so as to be able to pursue their own interests the more readily, or those who are at least not unwilling to have power thrust upon them if the situation should arise. Yet the emergence of a set of powerful individuals within the collegial body is not the irresistible consequence of a particular set of personality characteristics in the individuals concerned, though this is no doubt of importance in determining which particular individuals are able to achieve and maintain positions of influence.

The persistence and relative stability of power differentiation as a structural feature of a formally collegial body is only to be understood in structural terms. Social power is a matter of access to resources. It was the differential access to resources necessary to decision making and implementation that sustained the influence of the stratum of powerful individuals within the organization we studied. At least three sorts of resources relevant to the making and implementation of decisions can be distinguished.

1 First, and most obviously important, is specialist knowledge or expertise.[29] In the professional organization studied, however, this was not an important primary factor in power differentiation. On the contrary, the overtly collegial pattern of authority was based precisely on the fact that as fellow professionals all the members, at least of managerial status, were equal under this rubric.
2 Secondly, the control of plant, equipment or funds is an important 'material' resource which may be deployed subtly yet coercively to great effect. This was of most significance in the case of the managers of the general service departments, Accounts, Central Records, Establishments, Buildings and Works, and so forth. The control of material resources as a power base is obvious, and attempts to neutralize it may be institutionalized, though not always consciously. The general service departments for instance were specialized and distinguished from the professional departments, their staff did not enjoy the prestige of the professional workers who referred to them as 'mere administrators'. Though this neutralizing technique was not altogether successful by itself, however,[30] the discretion of the general service departments was usually closely watched by one or more of the sub-committees of the general management committee. The

successful operation of these committees indicates the importance of a further basis of power differentiation.

3 The third alternative lies in the access to structural resources or position in the decision-making system treated as a social network or communication grid. In particular, it underlines the importance of committee membership as a structural resource for the individual. Membership of one of the more powerful committees in turn conferred more power not merely in providing the opportunity to participate in more far-reaching decisions but in providing access to system-relevant information. In the context of the shadowy complexities of the involuted hierarchy, this alone secured for the professional the possibility of restricting the behaviour of other individuals or groups and at the same time legitimated it.[31]

Decision making in practice appeared to us to be a matter of who was able to produce an opportune statement at the right moment. A major element in this was the knowledge of how other committees would react. Frequently, the powerful sub-committees would be purposely represented on a subordinate committee. Sometimes, representation might occur by chance. But the importance of interlocking committee membership was great and incremental. The individual who achieved the position of link between committees need say little or nothing. The fact that he knew what another committee was doing would give weight to his presence, and his presumed activity in other relevant decision making would dispose fellow committee members to give him resources (if only their confidence and/or confidences) so that he would be able to operate on their behalf wherever else he did speak. The successful link man would seek to maintain this pluralistic ignorance, for every exercise of power is a potential revelation of its limitations. Not merely seniority nor experience on other committees qualified a departmental manager for election or co-option to the crucial policy-vetting sub-committees. Seniority and experience alone were insufficient. It was necessary that the qualifications be allied with discretion, a prudent tactfulness that in effect amounted to the capacity to preserve the opacity of the decision-making process. The involuted hierarchy provided the structural framework within which this was possible and to which it was functionally necessary. A tactless oligarch would be an obvious oligarch. An overt bid for influence would be rejected as unprofessional and thus a breach of the organization's institutional values of professional equality and autonomy. The professional ethic shared by the members of the collegial body committed them at least formally to mutual respect and confidence.[32] However, the individual who was able to marshal resources of system-relevant information was thereby qualified for nomination or co-option to more important committees. Sometimes, it seemed, the respect due to such managers in the field of their professional experience was also extended to their secondary expertise.

The paradox of efficiency

Operating in the public sector the organization studied was particularly vulnerable to demands for efficiency in the management of its resources and, at the same time, sensitive to criticism of its professional standards. In such a situation the rationality of administration and the autonomy of professional judgement may appear to be in conflict in so far as efficiency criteria impose non-professional constraints upon problems of professional practice. The emergent decision-making system we have been describing is the setting within which the dilemma was resolved.

Efficiency can only be evaluated in terms of the rationality of a specific means–end relationship. In respect of rapid decision making, the organization appears more efficient the further we leave behind the formal, collegial authority structure and approach the oligarchy which has evolved within it. The question therefore arises of why the outward and apparently unrealistic structure is nevertheless so strongly adhered to and why the micropolitics of the situation are not readily acknowledged.

The deployment of available resources and the maintenance of both the individual and collective autonomy of the professional staff are potentially in conflict. But at the same time they are essential to one another because the chief resource, though not the only one, the organization has to deploy is the trained judgement of its professional staff. Approximation to rationality in the pursuit of either efficiency of administration or the autonomy of expertise is self-defeating.[33] The dilemma is not an either/or problem but a matter of disparate goals which no group has yet been in a position to order into a preferential hierarchy.[34] The possibility that such an ordering may be imposed by the public authorities, to whom the concern is ultimately responsible, cannot be ruled out. This, we would argue, however, would be at the cost of an overall reduction in the effectiveness with which any of the goals could be pursued.

On the other hand, this is not to claim that the organization has necessarily achieved the best of all possible compromises between bureaucratization and professional autonomy. The particular accommodation of these goals which has been achieved is the outcome of the idiosyncratic history of the organization in question. It would in any case probably be modified by variations in size and by changes in extra-organizational constraints.

The involuted hierarchy and the balance of interests

The historical circumstances surrounding the emergence of the involuted hierarchy and the oligarchy implicit within it remain undocumented. It can, however, be functionally related to the interests of the professional workers in respect of both their status within the organization and their collective position *vis-à-vis* the outside world.

The organization's accountability to the external public authorities for the use of its funds together with the internal administrative exigencies consequent on the activities of the bureaucratically organized general service departments both, at least potentially, threaten the collective autonomy and individual discretion of the professionals. A collegial authority structure is not well adapted to meet this environmental pressure. As Weber argued, 'collegiality unavoidably obstructs the promptness of decision, the consistency of policy, the clear responsibility of the individual, and ruthlessness to outsiders in combination with the maintenance of discipline within the group'.[35]

The centralization of power in the hands of a small group of departmental managers thus circumvented most of the weaknesses of a collegial authority in a competitive environment. On the other hand, the powerful few could only act with authority while they maintained their equality of status with their professional colleagues. The structural resources from which their influence derived were the product of a committee structure made necessary by the equal claims to participation in decision making of all the professional departmental managers.

The fact that some departmental managers exercised a great deal more power than others was, of course, an open secret. But just how influential any one individual might be was very hard or impossible to establish. It was thus not only the interest of the already influential that preserved the opacity of the structure of intercursive power. While the involuted hierarchy of committees provided them with a ready means of diverting or avoiding criticism, it also served to protect the prestige of their fellow members of the collegial body.

At least as far as the majority of their colleagues was concerned, it was not clear whether or not any given departmental manager was able to influence at least indirectly a particular decision. The possibility that he could, could never be excluded. Impotence over any issue or range of issues was as veiled as effective power. Thus despite an effective differentiation of power, a belief in the community of equals could be sustained. Furthermore, it was not merely possible to reconcile the ethic of professional autonomy with the emergence in practice of a hierarchy of influence, but together with the consequent opacity of the decision-making process, the convention of respect for the discretion of fellow professionals was itself the basis on which the differentiation of power was founded.

Summary and discussion

In our description of a large organization staffed predominantly by professionals we have shown how the conflict between bureaucracy and the claims of professional autonomy has in practice been accommodated. This has been achieved within an elaborate and involuted system of committee control which has been able to exploit the uncertainties of collegial authority without destroying it. Indeed, it was the maintenance of the conventions of collegial authority which has provided the structural bases of the effective differentiation of power among fellow professionals.

The collective values of the organization's members, particularly those sustaining mutual respect and avoidance of overt criticism among professionals, have been an essential component of this pattern. The affirmation of collective values was encouraged by environmental pressures that threaten them. This served to obscure the real pattern of decision making in the organization rather than clarify it. The result has been to facilitate modifications in the power structure which may strengthen the collective interests of the professionals as a whole.

The structural model of power relations which emerges from this analysis suggests a number of possible directions for further research:

1 It should be possible to test the effect on this type of decision-making system of changes in size, in normative consensus, the availability of resources and the status of organizational publics.[36]
2 At the level of individual role-behaviour there are several questions which permit of further examination. For example, empirical studies have suggested that marginality between groups produces role-strain which is resolved by a compromise between situational exigencies and personal conscience.[37] Merton, of course, suggested in a theoretical discussion, that where the actual behaviour of the role-player is concealed from his reference-groups it is possible for him to play one off against another.[38] This is analogous to the maintenance of pluralistic ignorance by the successful committee link-man. It would be interesting to know why such a solution, with its attendant advantages, is not practised more frequently than recent studies of role-conflict suggest.
3 At a more general level our observations suggest that where it is necessary or desirable that status differentiation should be minimized, then it is probable that the power structure will remain opaque. Conversely, where the clarity and efficiency (in the bureaucratic sense) of decision-making processes is emphasized, then status differentiation must follow. Comparative studies in the structure of political power and social differentiation would be required to test the substantive truth of this hypothesis at the societal level.[39] This latter point indicates, some of the interest of the structural analysis we have developed in its relevance to a number of current issues in sociology.

Notes

1 D. Pugh and D. Hickson, 'The Comparative Study of Organization' in Denis Pym (ed.), *Industrial Society*, Pelican, London, 1968.
2 T. Burns and G. Stalker, *The Management of Innovation*, Tavistock, London, 1961.

3 Mason Haire (ed.), 'Biological Models and Empirical Histories in the Growth of Organizations' in *Modern Organization Theory*, John Wiley and Sons Inc., New York, 1959; B. Indik, 'Relation between Organization Size and the Supervision Ratio' in *Administrative Science Quarterly*, **9** (1964–5), 301–12.

4 Joan Woodward, *Industrial Organization*, Oxford University Press, Oxford, 1965.

5 See S. N. Eisenstadt, 'Bureaucracy and Bureaucratization', *Current Sociology*, **7**(2) (1958); Michel Crozier, *The Bureaucratic Phenomenon*, Tavistock, London, 1964.

6 Max Weber, *The Theory of Social and Economic Organization* (translated by A. Henderson and T. Parsons), Hodge, London, 1947.

7 Karl Mannheim, *Man in Society*, Kegan Paul, London, 1940.

8 Melville Dalton, 'Conflict Between Staff and Line Managerial Officers', *American Sociological Review*, **15** (1950), 342–51. Cf. M. K. Bacchus, 'Relationship between Professional and Administrative Officers in a Government Department', *Sociological Review*, **15**(2) (1967), 155–78.

9 *Op. cit.*, p. 65.

10 Morris Janowitz, 'Changing Patterns of Organizational Authority', *Administrative Science Quarterly*, **3** (1959), 473–93.

11 P. Blau and W. Scott, *Formal Organizations*, Routledge and Kegan Paul, 1962, p. 183. Cf. The findings of Pugh and Hickson, *op. cit.*, esp. pp. 392–3.

12 Cf. Pym, *op. cit.*, p. 100, and Mark Abrahamson, *The Professional in the Organization*, Chicago, Rand McNally, 1967, ch. I.

13 Ref., e.g. G. L. Millerson, *The Qualifying Associations: A Study in Professionalization*, Routledge and Kegan Paul, London, 1964; H. M. Vollmer and D. L. Mills (eds), *Professionalization*, Prentice-Hall, Englewood Cliffs, N.J., 1966; and W. Watson, 'Social Mobility and Social Class in Industrial Communities' in Max Gluckman (ed.), *Closed Systems and Open Minds*, Oliver and Boyd, Edinburgh, 1964.

14 R. Michels, *Political Parties* (translated by E. Paul and C. Paul), Dover Publications, New York, 1959.

15 Ibid.

16 *Op. cit.*, p. 310. Cf. the similarity with the position taken by the Donovan Commission. Thus, 'Many of those who conduct industrial relations in Britain are content with things as they are, because the arrangements are comfortable and flexible and provide a very high degree of self-government. Existing arrangements can be condemned only because these important benefits are outweighed by the disadvantages: the tendency of extreme decentralization and self-government to degenerate into indecision and anarchy; the propensity to breed inefficiency; and the reluctance of change. All these characteristics become damaging as they develop, as the rate of technical progress increases as the need for economic growth becomes more urgent.' *Report of the Royal Commission on Trade Unions and Employers' Associations 1965–1968*, Cmd. 3623, HMSO, London, 1968, para. 1018, p. 262.

17 *Op. cit.*, p. 308.

18 The organization had its own terminology for the various component parts of the management structure. The substitution of more general names and descriptions will we hope serve to emphasize the wider theoretical implications of the discussion to help the reader in observing parallels in other kinds of undertaking. In addition, we have been concerned to avoid any risk of embarrassment to members of the organization to which our account refers.

19 Cf. Sir Robert Aitken, *Administration of a University*, University of London Press,

London, 1966, with C. Carter, 'An Intolerable Degree of Complication', *Universities Quarterly*, **21**(2) (1966–7), 257–9.

20 E.g. T. Burns and G. Stalker, *op. cit.*

21 R. Michels, *op. cit.*

22 Max Weber, *op. cit.*, p. 366; cf. R. V. Clements, *Managers: A Study of Their Careers in Industry*, Allen and Unwin, London, 1958, p. 159; see also Report from the Select Committee on Education and Science, Session 1968–9. *Student Relations*, **1**, 449, paras 180–1.

23 On one occasion a decision on the erection of a temporary building announced in the report of a sub-committee to the general management committee led to an illuminating jurisdiction dispute between the members of four different sub-committees. This took the form of a sort of caucus-race. The right of any of these committees to a say on the matter was denied by no one. Speakers on all sides claimed only that their own sub-committee had a right to submit advice to the others before they reached a decision.

24 R. Cyert and J. March, *A Behavioural Theory of the Firm*, Prentice-Hall, Englewood Cliffs, N.J., 1963, and H. A. Simon, 'On the Concept of Organizational Goal', *Administrative Science Quarterly*, **9**(1) (1964–5), 1–22.

25 Clements argues that for the managers, decision making may not take place in the usual sense, many decisions are 'rendered inevitable by their own and other people's actions'. *Op. cit.*, p. 159, and compare René Cutforth, p. 12, *The Listener*, 2 January 1969.

26 Intercursive power relationships exist between groups or their members and should be distinguished from integral power, which term describes the institutional power of a group or society over and against the private interests of its members. Ref. J. A. A. Van Doorn, 'Sociology and the Problem of Power', *Sociologica Nederlandica*, **1** (1962–3), pp. 16ff., and cf. Tom Burns, 'Micropolitics', *Administrative Science Quarterly*, **6**(3) (1961–2), 257–81.

27 Cf. C. Northcote Parkinson, *Parkinson's Law*, John Murray, London, 1958.

28 Ref. Van Doorn, *op. cit.*, p. 12, who defines power as 'the possibility on the part of a person or group to restrict other persons or groups in the choice of their behaviour, in performance of his or its purposes'.

29 Other than those listed under (2).

30 Ref. John P. Speigel, 'The Resolution of Role Conflict within the Family', ch. 29 in N. W. Bell and E. A. Vogel (eds), *A Modern Introduction to the Family*, The Free Press, New York, 1960, and cf. Bacchus, *op cit.*

31 This was above all true in the case of the general management committee's full-time executive chairman. Cf. the position of a university vice-chancellor as described by Rowland Eustace in 'The Government of Scholars' in D. A. Martin (ed.), *Anarchy and Culture*, Routledge and Kegan Paul, London, 1969, p. 54.

32 Informally, however, the role of gossip in the culture of the organization should not be overlooked; ref. Max Gluckman, 'Gossip and Scandal', *Current Anthropology*, **4**(3) (1963), 307–16, and Tom Burns, *Industrial Man*, chapter entitled 'On the Plurality of Social Systems', Penguin, Harmondsworth, 1969, p. 234.

33 Cf. Sir Robert Aitken, *op. cit.*, and N. J. Demerath, R. W. Stephens and R. R. Taylor, *Power, Presidents and Professors*, London and New York, Basic Books, 1967.

34 H. A. Simon, *op. cit.*, and Brian H. Loasby, 'The Decision Maker in the Organization', *Journal of Management Studies*, **5**(3), (1968), 352–64.

35 *Op. cit.*, p. 39.

36 P. Blau and W. R. Scott, *op. cit.*, ch. 3.
37 N. Gross, W. S. Mason and A. W. McEachern, *Explorations in Role Analysis*, New York, Wiley, 1958. Sam Stouffer and J. Toby, 'Role Conflict and Personality', *American Journal of Sociology*, **56**(5) (1950–51), 395–406. P. Sutcliffe and M. Haberman, 'Factors Influencing Choice in Role Conflict Situations', *American Sociological Review*, **21**(6) (1956), 695–703.
38 R. K. Merton, 'The Role Set', *British Journal of Sociology*, **8**(3) (1957), 106–20.
39 Cf. I. Vallier, 'Structural Differentiation, Production Imperatives and Communal Norms: the Kibbutz in Crisis', *Social Forces*, **40**(3) (1961–2), 233–42.

5
Towards the collegial primary school

Jim Campbell

[. . .]

An image of the 'collegial' primary school

The contemporary image of good practice has been promoted by the Inspectorate since 1978. [. . .] It is of the 'collegial' primary school, predicated on the two values of *teacher collaboration* and *subject expertise*. [. . .] It has a number of characteristic features. It shows small working groups of teachers reporting back recommendations for school-wide change to the collectivity of the whole staff meeting for decision taking. These groups are led and organized by the curriculum postholders, who draw upon expertise from outside school as well as upon their own professional knowledge, in order to enable the staff to develop the curriculum as authoritatively as possible. Occasionally, the postholder works alongside class teachers to illustrate ideas in practice, and to become aware of progress throughout the school. The skills involved in these processes are not only academic; considerable sensitivity, personal enthusiasm and charm are required in order to maintain good working relationships in schools where professional practice is being subjected to the scrutiny of colleagues. The teachers involved become used to tolerating uncertainty and working under pressure of time and conflicting demands. Supporting this collaborative effort is the headteacher who has committed himself or herself to devolving responsibility to the staff group; servicing their activities by putting appropriate school facilities, and where possible his or her time, at their disposal.

The image also shows an atmosphere, ethos or climate distinctive to collegiality. The teachers exist in a school in which constructive and critical scrutiny of each other's practice and ideas is the normal expectation. There is a continuing commitment to professional development through in-service activities both within the school and outside it. Although the teachers are not insensitive to the implications of such involvement for their own career prospects, the major focus of in-service training is the whole school, and there is an open understanding that teachers will feed back into school implications they see for their colleagues of off-site in-service courses. The ethos is not created simply by encouraging teachers to feel solidarity with one another, but by deliberate strategies that make role expectations explicit to all staff, and by the head's involvement in school-based development in practical and supportive ways that do not undermine the authority of teachers with special expertise. The overt commitment to evaluate their initiative collec-tively accustoms the teachers to giving accounts to each other of the reasons and justifications for particular approaches to the curriculum, and so helps them to anticipate representing their subject or subject area to people outside the school, to parents, other teachers in feeder schools, to advisers, and governors and others. The school thus becomes collectively accountable for its curriculum. The teachers committed to collegiality see the atmosphere in the school as the element most critical to its maintenance, and derive strong personal and professional satisfactions from their involvement in, and con-tribution to, its continuance. They see the creation and maintenance of such an atmosphere as the responsibility not just of the headteacher, but of the whole staff group. Collegiality will survive the departure of the head.

It is obvious that the foregoing is a projection from empirical reality, not a description of it. [. . .] In the foreground of this image is not the school's organization, or children's emotional adjustment, or community rela-tionships, but working groups of teachers engaged in the process of develop-ing school-wide policies and practices for the curriculum.

There is some evidence from the USA that the cluster of in-school variables depicted above as collegiality, is related to effective change. Goodlad (1975) analysed a 5-year action research programme designed to encourage primary schools to improve their curriculum from within. He characterized the processes involved as DDAE – dialogue, decision making, action and evaluation – and reported on a 'league' of schools cooperating in the research. In those schools scoring high on DDAE, there were more 'co-operative teaching groups, more friendship networks amongst staff, and more task-oriented communication networks amongst staff. Teachers had more influence in decision-making, especially in areas affecting schools as total units' and heads of such schools were more 'apt to see teacher influence in schools as a desirable condition'.

There is an element of tautology in the defining characteristics of the schools, but Goodlad concluded that high DDAE was associated with high teacher morale, a high sense of professionalism and a high sense of the teacher's own power among staff, especially where there were effectively functioning 'sub-groups' of staff. If these characteristics were combined, 'they helped us . . . to describe a school's propensity for change, a school's readiness for and ability to work towards self improvement' (Goodlad, 1975, p. 135).

In-school obstacles to the development of collegiality

Drawing an ideal picture, however helpful it is as an expression of values, none the less immediately raises questions, especially perhaps for teachers who find the values attractive. These questions are about obstacles to change, and the extent to which practice in contemporary primary schools may be hindered from moving to a better match with the image, if teachers become committed to the values it embodies.

Two features of the culture of contemporary primary schools in particular may hinder the development of collegiality: *role relationships* between teachers, and the *conditions* in which teachers work. The former has been seen in much of the literature as the overriding factor. Until very recently, the latter has been virtually ignored. I believe that the evidence for the problems associated with role relationships is rather insubstantial and to some extent dated, and that the major stumbling block for collegiality is no longer teacher relationships, but some of the conditions in which primary schoolteachers have to work, which are not conducive to curriculum development of a school-based kind.

Role relations in primary schools

Studies of role relationships in primary schools by Lortie (1969), Taylor *et al.* (1974) and Coulson (1974, 1976, 1978) have drawn attention to the relationship between heads and class teachers, noting the dominant power position, both in law and in convention, of the former in the structure of school staff roles. However, the important common feature of these studies is not the relative *positions* in the structure of schools, but the complementary sets of *attitudes* that heads and teachers have towards each other. The attitudes support the conventional power positions and give them life and meaning.

On the part of the headteacher, these attitudes combine into 'paternalism', according to Coulson's (1976) analysis, and include influencing teachers to adopt his own aims and methods, filtering information from outside the school, and protecting teachers from parents, and pupils from moral contamination. The explanation for this set of attitudes is the 'ego-identification' of the head with 'his' school, and the historical roots of the moral character of the role, according to Bernbaum (1976) and Peters (1976). On the part of the class teachers, the characteristic attitude set is 'acquiescence' in subordination to the head's dominance, partly because of 'immersion in teaching tasks', according to Coulson, to such an extent that they are 'relatively indifferent to organisational matters involving the school as a whole'. These attitudes preserve a kind of mutual autonomy in preferred professional activities. Heads are in charge of what they like to call 'their' school, and teachers are in charge of 'their' class. By a proprietorial and implicit gift exchange, the head offers not to interfere in the classroom and the class teachers accept as their part of the bargain not to expect to participate in school-wide policy making. Thereby, both parties gain *de facto* control over what gives them most professional satisfaction.

From the point of view of collegiality, these studies, which have helped to create the prevailing view of primary teaching, have identified three major problems. First, class teachers get very great personal and professional satisfaction from the arena most in their own control – their classroom. Leese (1978) illustrated the point in graphic terms:

> a teacher's real gratification comes from what her pupils do and learn with her. . . . There is I think, no greater reward for my daughter, a first grade (i.e. reception class) teacher than the evidence that those who come to her unable to read can do so when they leave. There is a strong interpersonal transaction and subsequent bond between her and each child. It is her individual influence upon her client which makes her professional. . . . Consequently she deeply resents and resists those who would stylize and interfere with that intimate art upon which her ego rests . . .

To put those satisfactions at risk by subjecting them to a more public scrutiny, and to allocate energy and commitment to more collaborative endeavours outside the classroom, is not self-evidently seductive for already effective teachers, and not at all so for ineffective ones.

Secondly, for all concerned in the primary school, the conventional role perceptions are comfortable. They function to insulate class teachers and headteachers from each other and thus from the considerable opportunities for conflict that might arise if they stepped outside the normal role expectations into the less clearly defined authority territory of 'whole-school' activities. These arrangements make for what Hanson (1977) has called predictability in role relationships. Activities involving collective discussion and decision making reduce predictability and require tolerance of ambiguity and conflict in relationships, and this is not a very comfortable experience, especially in relatively small organizations, where daily and frequent face-to-face contacts require that friction be avoided as far as possible. Thus there is in the conventional role relationships a subtle but potent pressure to settle for what you know you can do well rather than enter the high-risk enterprise of school-based development.

A third problem derives from teacher attitudes to authority; according to Lortie, primary school teachers are disinclined to recognize any authority intermediate between themselves and the head. Coulson (1976) and Coulson and Cox (1975) showed that class teachers did not accept decisions arrived at by deputies and postholders, but sought clearance from the head before going along with them. Curriculum postholders trying to lead staff groups and basing their leadership on their post of responsibility, or on their expertise, will thus be operating in what is perceived as no-man's-land, where territorial rights are in question, and boundaries in dispute.

Alexander (1984), in a major critical reworking that questions the Lortie/Coulson thesis, illustrates the persistence of paternalism and acquiescence by means of a metaphor that the modern consciousness will find provocative. According to it, primary school relationships are like those in a Victorian family, with its dominant male head and its submissive and subordinate, mostly female, members, each happy to perform her allotted function at the head's behest. Alexander acknowledges the problem posed by female heads of infant schools (though not by the ubiquitous overly deferential male teacher in junior schools), but the metaphor itself encapsulates the prevailing cultural analysis in a potent manner.

This analysis shows the primary school world pressing upon class teachers to settle for restricted professionality of the classroom practice, leaving the extended role of curriculum policy making to the head; it sets the sure and personal satisfactions of the private classroom experience with pupils, against the uncertain and stressful public arena of staff meetings and collaborative groups. It leads heads and class teachers to seek comfortable roles of relative independence from, rather than interdependence upon, each other. In the prevailing view, the primary school culture is predicated on individualistic, not collective, endeavour. As Lawson (1979) has suggested about the primary school world from the pupil's point of view, fraternity is not a dominant value. For the pursuit of collegiality, a more daunting scenario would be difficult to imagine.

A reappraisal of the prevailing view

The view of the professional culture of the primary school as massively oppositional to the development of more collegial relationships, needs to be questioned on two grounds: the nature of the evidence upon which it has been based, and some very recent studies that suggest that teacher roles, or at least teacher perceptions of their roles, may be changing in the direction whereby collegiality could become more feasible.

The empirical basis for the prevailing view is rather insubstantial for making any general statement about teacher relationships in contemporary primary schools. Lortie's study was of US elementary schools in the late 1960s. Taylor and his colleagues used questionnaires from 120 teachers in 12 schools rated as typical by local authority advisers. Although it is unclear precisely when the questionnaires were completed, the study itself was published in 1974. The authors were careful to describe the study as 'exploratory', and urged the need for more real-life detail created from case studies of actual schools. Coulson's (1976, 1978) analyses were derived from his Master's thesis, presented in 1974, which investigated the conceptions of the deputy head's role held by heads and deputies, again by questionnaire although with a large (more than 600) sample. He argued for administrative change in the direction of expertise and collegiality and the use of flexible working groups led by 'the best qualified and expert person in the subject area the group is to tackle, regardless of his position in the school' (Coulson, 1976, p. 105).

The first point, therefore, is that the influential studies were using material gathered in the late 1960s and early 1970s, so that none relates to teachers' perceptions since the Great Debate, or more importantly, to the time following the publication of the Primary Survey. Wicksteed and Hill's (1979) survey suggests that teacher attitudes to classroom autonomy have changed, in ways that may soon make the earlier studies period pieces. Secondly, strictly speaking, the studies were of what teachers wrote about primary school teaching on questionnaires, not of teaching itself as experienced in the real worlds of classroom, staffroom and playground. Such a methodology loses out on the diversity and complexity of the real-life situations from which they are abstracted. Thirdly, there is no claim that the samples were representative, either of schools generally, or of good practice, or of anything else, with the ambiguous exception of Taylor's 'typical' or 'modal' schools (which seems to mean that they were not regarded by advisers as unusual in terms of intake, resourcing, degree of innovation and quality of home–school contacts). Thus, strictly speaking again, the studies tell us only what an identified number of particular teachers perceive, or believe about the culture of a particular number of schools, and relationships in them. Finally, both the English studies concluded that the existing teacher–headteacher relationships were anachronistic and in need of modification. Alexander's (1984) commentary on the issue goes further and sharply points out the 'fine line' between a class teacher's insistence on classroom autonomy for personal satisfactions, and 'mere self indulgence or professional irresponsibility'.

None of the above should be seen as criticizing the early studies for claiming to be more than could be justified. Their authors were scrupulous in indicating the nature and quality of their basic data. But the clarification of the nature of the evidence raises questions about how generalizable, how reliable and how dated the analysis conveyed in the studies is, in respect of contemporary primary schools. Some more recent studies suggest that primary school culture has begun to allow a little more flexibility than the somewhat tightly prescribed roles discerned in the earlier studies, whereas others suggest that teachers' perceptions and beliefs about the legitimacy of intermediate authority roles, such as postholders, are undergoing change.

[. . .]

A study sponsored by the Schools Council and the Primary Schools Research and Development Group at Birmingham University (1983) examined 'responsibility and the use of expertise' in primary schools using a range of methodologies, including questionnaires, interviews, discussion groups, free accounts and diaries, in order to obtain both range and depth in teacher perceptions and experience of the use of teacher expertise in schools. The study captured in a welcome and unusual way, a diverse and even contradictory range of teacher perceptions about the issues. It revealed

teachers' unease about terms like 'expert' and even 'influence', while record-
ing their readiness to seek advice from postholders, especially in informal
ways. Non-postholders seemed more ready to acknowledge a distinctive role
for 'experts' in school, at least in interview. Headteachers on the whole
welcomed the idea of making fuller use of teacher expertise, with 80% of the
65 heads who completed a questionnaire approving of the Primary Survey's
suggestions to that effect (though they did not, ironically, seem to acknowledge their own self-interest, recognized by class teachers in interviews who
felt that postholders were still seen as 'instruments of the head; to do his
bidding, to realize his vision'). The heads also commented on the 'need for
staff to be engaged in a common enterprise. To co-operate as a team, perhaps
through small committees co-ordinated by staff with special curricular
interests . . .' The 465 teachers who responded to a questionnaire perceived
as very or extremely important sources of their own professional development, 'help from colleagues with special knowledge and experience'
(89.7%), and 'help from teachers with scale posts of responsibility' (82.6%).

Paradoxically, although these teachers strongly supported the idea of
school-based in-service activity, they did not expect teachers with posts of
responsibility to be engaged in 'chairing a group of colleagues working in a
curriculum area'. An important finding was that there were subject differences in the extent to which teachers would wish to draw upon subject
expertise of colleagues, and in the kind of help that would be sought. There
was more readiness to look for help in drawing-up schemes of work, than in
teaching methods, resource management and methods of assessment, possibly because the first area is seen as school policy, whereas the other three are
seen as classroom practice. The teachers on the whole thought the wider use
of teacher expertise would be mainly beneficial to the school, and judged that
its effectiveness would depend to a great extent upon school-wide support.
The ambivalent nature of support for the idea in general was summed up by
the authors:

> One way teachers had of seeing the teacher expert was as an agent of
> change, alert to innovations in primary education and determined to
> make a contribution to the professional development of his colleagues.
> Another, as a quietly concerned colleague, ready to help if asked.
> In the main it was the last way of seeing teacher expert that was most
> generally supported. The former found more support among teachers
> with posts of responsibility and among teachers who belong to a
> teaching association. But this support, though evident, was not strong.
> (Primary Schools Research and Development Group/
> Schools Council, 1983, p. 98.)

The evidence from the Birmingham study does not reveal a profession
wholeheartedly committed to changing conventional authority roles and
relationships; in many ways it could be used to demonstrate that teachers are
divided about the consequences for in-school relationships of implementing

the recommendations of the Primary Survey. I interpret it, tentatively, as a record of a profession at a transitional stage, aware of the potential benefit to a school of a shift in exercise of authority to teachers with subject expertise, but perceptive about the repercussions on the quality of staff relationships, and fearful of a loss of informality and reciprocity in professional exchanges. But the study cannot easily be used to argue that teacher perceptions of their roles are fixed in the immutable 'class teacher–headteacher' division of earlier studies.

A study at Durham University by Rodger *et al.* (1983) comprised case studies of teachers with posts of responsibility built up collaboratively by the postholders and Rodger, by self-monitoring, triangulated interviews with the postholders and their headteachers, diaries, analysis of critical incidents and a questionnaire. The case studies are rich in personal detail and embedded in the contextual minutiae of postholders' working worlds, offering fascinating source material for examining the potential and problems associated with changing teacher roles in the contemporary primary school. There is naturally great variation in the case studies, but the general picture gained from them supports the view of a professional culture being slowly and with difficulty modified in the direction of greater collegiality with some enlightened headteachers enabling postholders to attempt to influence the work of other class teachers, without challenging the principle of class teaching itself. The conclusion of Rodger's study noted the interdependence of the roles of postholder and head and the increase in 'corporate' approaches to managing aspects of the curriculum. He concluded, as the Birmingham study did, that postholders preferred informal 'consultant' roles to more directive ones, because they were uneasy at the prospect of being required to operate as a 'leader' in contexts where their colleagues felt themselves equally competent.

[. . .]

Caution is necessary, given small, untypical samples, but these recent studies have findings about role relationships in primary schools that point, albeit uncertainly, in the direction of collegiality and away from individualistic roles in private and autonomous classrooms.

Teachers' conditions of work

A second obstacle to collegiality is a more practical one, and concerns the conditions in which teachers work. For the purposes of this analysis, I am restricting the definition of working conditions to (a) the provision of *time*, and (b) access to *facilities* and *ideas* for in-school development.

The use of teacher time

[. . .]

Rodger *et al.* (1983, p. 108) comment of one of their postholders:

Organisation of non-contact time. Fiona was never anything but totally dissatisfied with this aspect of her role. She either had no non-contact time due to circumstances in the school, or it was taken up with the remnants of her previous post, e.g. games and coaching. Accordingly she never felt able to devote enough time to her curricular leadership function.

In the conclusions of this study, Rodger *et al.* indicated ways in which their postholders had 'won' time from other activities. These included such strategies as doubling up classes with another postholder and using hymn practices, assemblies, visits from outside speakers, etc., as well as team teaching and having the head teach classes (p. 136). Whatever their immediate effectiveness, such strategies required the teachers to remove themselves from school activities in which they would normally participate. The assumptions about teacher time underlying curricular leadership activities thus appeared to clash with assumptions about teacher time underlying 'normal' teaching and teaching-related activities.

A fuller consideration of the issues raised by this kind of clash is offered below, where the use of teacher time is discussed under four headings – '*other contact*' time, '*group*' time, '*snatched*' time and '*personal*' time.

1 '*Other contact* time. The first kind of time is what is normally (and inappropriately) referred to as 'non-contact' time. This is time formally provided in the school to enable the teacher to be free of class teaching. [. . .] From the point of view of curriculum development, this time might most usefully serve two purposes, namely working alongside colleagues to develop ideas in practice or monitoring work through the school, and visiting other schools, or resource agencies in the LEA and elsewhere, in order to increase expertise.

There are two points to make about the 'other contact' time. First, [. . .] there is very little of it available for through-school and outside-school activities of this kind. [. . .] Secondly, non-contact time is a strangely inflexible arrangement, since it means that the postholder is free at a given time each week, whereas through-school development requires a much more flexible response. Some weeks there will be no need, from a curriculum development point of view, for postholders to be freed from teaching their classes. Some weeks they will need to work alongside teachers at quite different times from other weeks, and on occasions they will need to be out of school for a morning or a day. It is thus not merely shortage of time for this role that is the problem, but arrangements that are inappropriately inflexible to suit the curricular leadership function. [. . .]

2 *Group time.* A second category is 'group time', i.e. time spent in working groups, of varying size, including both the smaller review and development groups producing guidelines, etc., and the whole staff groups which arrive at decisions about through-school policies. The current conditions mean that teachers have to organize these activities, obviously, outside the

times when pupils are being taught. This means either at lunchtimes or after school, when most children have gone home, or on [. . .] days given over to in-service training.

[. . .] Many primary schoolteachers conventionally give time both over the lunch break and after school to pupils, for example by organizing clubs, music, sports and games coaching, extra reading and language work, etc. This means that curriculum working groups may interfere with these activities, or that some teachers, often the most committed ones, will be unable to participate in them, or will do so intermittently. Although this problem can be mitigated to some extent by advance planning, there would be understandable resistance among primary school teachers if in-school development was to be implemented at the expense of time devoted to these other kinds of professional activities. [. . .]

3 *'Snatched' time.* A third time category is what can only be called 'snatched' time. Much school-based work involves informal discussion and consultation. [. . .] It is clear from both the Birmingham and the Durham studies that class teachers value very highly curricular leadership exercised informally, but the use of snatched time for considering curricular issues must look to outsiders as an amateurish way for professional affairs to be conducted. It is probably necessary to make distinctions according to the nature of such consultations; a brief word over coffee about how to start pupils off on using pastels may be sensible and desirable given the informal and friendly nature of most staffroom contacts, but discussion of possible problems and approaches in a suggested scheme of work needs a less harried, more thoughtful context than a school corridor or classroom. [. . .]

4 *'Personal' time.* The final category is 'personal time', i.e. time used by individuals for curriculum development, entirely out of school, either for reading, attending courses, and time used for discussion with external 'experts' such as university and college tutors. [. . .]

Official recognition of the problem of teacher time
[. . .]

[. . .] Evidence from national surveys is beginning to identify teacher time as a major problem. It emerged clearly in two recent reports by HMI (DES, 1983a, b), one concerned with 9–13 middle schools, and one with secondary schools.

In the middle schools, postholders had on average 3¼ hours per week for curricular and other responsibilities, allocated free from teaching. Despite this, HMI raised teacher time as an issue for discussion, seeing the level of staffing in the schools leaving:

> little margin of teacher time for purposes other than the teaching of a class. . . . While it is reasonable to expect teachers to give some personal time to planning work, managing resources and keeping up to

date with developments, they also need sufficient opportunities, while the schools are in session, to observe the work the children are doing and to guide and support other teachers. A very heavy teaching load inevitably limits their effectiveness as consultants or co-ordinators.

(DES, 1983a, para. 8.13)

In the secondary schools report there had been a co-ordinated attempt to adopt 'curriculum appraisal' in some 34 schools in five authorities. The Inspectors found that 'radical thinking about the curriculum was difficult to realize because teachers had to maintain the necessary daily routines', and in an explicit reference to teacher time, pointed out both the conflict of priorities and the resource implications.

Much of the discussion and group planning had to take place at the end of a full day's teaching, and this was not the best time for the considered discussion of important issues . . . teachers were often prevented from giving a full commitment to the work (of curriculum development) because of the routine pressures associated with their normal duties. Problems of communication within the schools have been accentuated by the limited time which is available for this work in the normal context of school life. If LEAs wish to sponsor work of this kind there are implications for staffing and in-service work.

(DES 1983b, p. 16)

The enterprise developed out of thoughtful and well-resourced collaboration between HMI, LEAs and teachers in schools that are staffed, as are 9–13 middle schools, more favourably than primary schools. If it partly foundered upon the problem of teacher time, it shows how important an issue it is for the profession as a whole to face up to in extending the movement for in-school development to the less formally resourced and supported context of the normal primary school.

Access to facilities and ideas

By facilities and ideas for in-school development I mean access to secretarial help, to reprographic processes, and to ideas and materials relevant to a particular programme.

Facilities

In most primary schools provision of facilities for reproducing notes or minutes of working group meetings, to ensure distribution of them in time for proper consideration, is antediluvian. To struggle for half an hour to get an antiquated Banda machine to provide even rough and ready versions of a manuscript original is a common experience; to have a secretary to type out and photocopy such matter is 'like gold', as one postholder said.

Conventional assumptions about the work of primary school teachers are that they will teach – they will be the 'teacher as teacher', and for that role all they will need is teaching materials, felt-tip pens for their work cards, and a ready supply of chalk. However, the 'teacher as educationalist' role requires of them that they produce working drafts, discussion papers, guidelines, and all the documentary trappings that flow from more collective forms of decision making. [. . .] Facilities in general are inadequate to cope with the kind of demands that in-school development has to make on secretarial and clerical services. [. . .]

Ideas and materials

A second problem is one of access to ideas and materials that can help in the curriculum development programme itself, and in the teachers' own professional development. [. . .] On the whole, teachers do not have easy access to recent thinking, relevant research and reports of practice in other schools, or even to information about where such ideas might be available. [. . .] The idea of a professional reference library in primary school staffrooms may sound a little pretentious, but easy access to major reports on the curriculum, together with teachers' handbooks on the major curriculum projects and materials in the normal curriculum areas, and subscription to one or two professionally oriented journals might go some way towards reducing the professional isolation of primary school staff. [. . .]

Teachers also need access to specialized advice on ideas and materials from outside the school, from advisers, university staff and other people. At the present time such access is difficult to arrange, mainly because it has not been given attention. It would be a considerable boost to schools involved in curriculum development if they knew that they could get access legitimately and quickly to the kinds of information and ideas necessary for its initiation and maintenance.

Conclusion

Obstacles to the full realization of collegiality in the professional life of primary schools have been examined in this chapter under the two headings of role relationships and working conditions. In the early 1970s, it was the relationships between teachers that were seen as the major obstacle to change, whereas the working conditions of teachers were not given much attention. If the very recent studies prove reliable guides, problems of teacher relationships and teacher perceptions of their roles appear to be reducing (though by no means disappearing) as the profession responds to pressure from HMI and others, and begins to accord recognition to the intermediate authority of postholders.

Teacher working conditions, however, seem stuck on the anachronistic

assumptions that there is no need to provide time, facilities and ideas for curriculum development. It is this aspect of primary school life that requires urgent reappraisal, especially in the light of findings of the most recent HMI surveys (DES, 1983a, b). At the present time, expectations for school-based curriculum development of the kind called for in the stream of documents from the DES are probably only realizable in those schools that have a fortunate combination of an enlightened and supportive headteacher and unusually talented and hard-working postholders. What is now required is that such development should become routinized in the system; it should be translated from the pioneering schools into the normal ones. [. . .]
[. . .]

References

Alexander, R. (1984). *Primary Teaching*. Eastbourne: Holt, Rinehart and Winston.
Bernbaum, G. (1976). 'The role of the head'. *In* Peters, R. S. (ed.), *The Role of the Head*. London: Routledge and Kegan Paul.
Coulson, A. A. (1974). *The deputy head in the primary school: The role conceptions of heads and deputy heads*. M.Ed. dissertation, University of Hull.
Coulson, A. A. (1976). 'The role of the primary head'. *In* Peters, R. S. (ed.), *The Role of the Head*. London: Routledge and Kegan Paul.
Coulson, A. A. (1978). 'The politics of curriculum reform'. *In* Richards, C. (ed.), *Power and the Curriculum*. Driffield: Nafferton Books.
Coulson, A. A. and Cox, M. (1975). 'What do deputies do?' *Education 3–13*, **3**(2), 100–103.
Department of Education and Science (1978). *Primary Education in England*. A survey by HMI. London: HMSO.
Department of Education and Science (1983a). *9–13 Middle Schools: An Illustrative Survey by HMI*. London: HMSO.
Department of Education and Science (1983b). *Curriculum 11–16: Towards a Statement of Entitlement*. London: HMSO.
Goodlad, J. I. (1975). *The Dynamics of Educational Change*. New York: McGraw-Hill.
Hanson, M. (1977). 'Beyond the bureaucratic model: A study of power and autonomy in educational decision making'. *Inter-change*, **7**(2). Quoted in Coulson (1978).
Lawson, K. (1979). 'The politics of primary school curricula'. *Education 3–13*, **7**(1), 23–7.
Leese, J. (1978). 'Politics and power in curriculum reform'. *In* Richards, C. (ed.), *Power and the Curriculum*. Driffield: Nafferton Books.
Lortie, D. (1969). 'The balance of control and autonomy in elementary school teaching'. *In* Etzioni, A. (ed.), *The Semi-professions and the Organisation*. New York: Free Press.
Peters, R. S. (ed.) (1976). *The Role of the Head*. London: Routledge and Kegan Paul.
Rodger, I. *et al.* (1983). *Teachers with Posts of Responsibility in Primary Schools*. Schools Council, University of Durham School of Education.
Schools Council (1983). *Primary Practice*. London: Methuen.

6
Building a political model

J. V. Baldridge

Theoretical sources of the political model

Three theoretical sources have been used for building a new political interpretation of university governance. First, the sociological tradition of 'conflict theory' seemed ripe for application to organizations. Secondly, it became
more and more apparent that the political dynamics of the university were
similar to those studied by 'community power' theorists in political science.
Thirdly, the so-called 'informal groups' approach in organization theory was
a good framework for analyzing the activities of interest groups as they
fought for influence. Each of these theoretical positions has greatly influenced
the political model, and it seems worthwhile to examine them briefly.

Conflict theory

In recent years a body of theoretical thought, characterized as 'conflict
theory', has been growing in sociology. Conflict theory has actually been a
major part of sociological analysis at least since Marx, but there has been a
revival of interest in this approach to social behavior in recent decades.
Marx's analysis, of course, centered on the social conflicts in industrializing
England, while Ralf Dahrendorf, Lewis Coser and others have extended the
same conflict analysis to the modern society.[1]* Many conflict ideas proposed
for the larger society can be applied to the smaller social system of an
organization. Several points of analysis are critical to this orientation. First,
conflict theorists emphasize the fragmentation of social systems into interest
groups, each with its own particular goals. Secondly, conflict theorists study
the interaction of these different interest groups and especially the conflict

*Superscript numerals refer to numbered notes at the end of this chapter.

processes by which one group tries to gain advantages over another. Thirdly, interest groups cluster around divergent values, and the study of the conflicting interests is a key part of the analysis. Finally, the study of change is a central feature of the conflict approach, for change is to be expected if the social system is fragmented by divergent values and conflicting interest groups.

The research concentrates on applying conflict theory to the university setting. Instead of looking at stability, we shall examine change; instead of looking for common values, we shall examine divergent values held by various groups; instead of emphasizing consensus, we shall examine the dynamics of conflict; instead of focusing on the integration of the whole system, we shall stress the role of interest groups as they disturb the system. Taken together, these conflict emphases provide one set of undergirding principles for building a new model.

The community power studies

A second scholarly tradition useful for understanding the 'political' university is the literature on community power. For several decades sociologists and political scientists have studied power articulation in American communities. Again and again these scholars have charted the complex processes by which various groups in the community influence governmental policy. The students of community power tried to map the distribution of power in the community and in the process they showed how the fragmented, complicated political scene is welded together by a multitude of political processes. Floyd Hunter's *Community Power Structure* and Robert Dahl's *Who Governs?* are classic studies in this field.[2]

Several of the community power emphases are useful for organizational analysis. First, one of the prime objectives of the community power theorists was a study of the *nature of power* in the political system. What kinds of power are available and how are they articulated? A second emphasis was on the role of *interest groups* in the political arena.[3] The theoretical and empirical research by political scientists is a vast reservoir of knowledge that can be tapped for studying interest groups in universities.

A third emphasis adopted from the community power theorists is a stress on *goal-setting activities*. In the past, many organization theorists have concentrated on 'efficiency', that is, on improving the technical *means* by which the organization carries out its goals. In fact, in the popular mind the 'efficiency expert' was the predominant image of the organization theorist. This is not difficult to understand, as most of the previous research was done in industrial organizations where the goals were clearly set. The real problem was determining how best to accomplish those predetermined goals. The most commonly studied organizations – business, industry and governmental agencies – were similar in their high degree of 'goal-specificity'. The role of organization theory for these organizations was to improve efficiency and cut costs, but rarely to confront the problem of goal selection.

The community power theorists can help us break out of this kind of provincialism, for they deal with political communites with very diffuse, differentiated goal-systems. For them it is senseless to deal only with efficiency in technical means, for the goals themselves are ambiguous, contested and changing. The political system is clearly a situation in which goal-setting activities are paramount. Because the university is similar to the goal-diffuse local community, we can fruitfully adopt the community power theorists' emphasis on goal-setting activities, as well as their stress on interest groups and the conflict between such groups.

Interest groups in organizations

A political interpretation of the university must deal with organizational interest groups, and among the best studies of this type is research done on prisons. There are strong pressures in a prison that promote the formation of militant interest groups. On the inside, the sharp cleavages between the prisoners and their captors make conflict the normal state of affairs. Powerful groups form on every side to fight for privileges and favors. On the outside, there are strong sentiments about the prison and numerous community groups try to influence its operation. Interest groups may take a variety of forms, some calling for stricter punishment, others demanding more rehabilitation, and still others investigating alleged mismanagement. The prison studies, then, are an excellent source for the study of organizational interest groups.[4]

A second body of organizational interest group studies has come largely from industrial settings. By and large these studies have focused on the man-to-man interaction patterns that develop within a peer group, and thus they are not particularly helpful for developing the interest group theme. However, a few have focused on the influence that the peer group exercises on the larger organization. The classic work by Roethlisberger and Dickson sometimes shifted attention away from the operation of the peer group itself to the influence that the group might have on the organization by restriction of work and violation of work rules. Most of the writing in this 'human relations' tradition devoted some attention to the group's influence on the total organization, but this was seldom their prime concern.[5] More recently, Melville Dalton applied this orientation quite successfully to industrial settings by emphasizing the informal group cleavages and their effects on the whole organization.[6]

A third source of insights into organizational interest groups is the excellent work of Phillip Selznick in *TVA and the Grass Roots*.[7] Selznick provides a vivid interpretation of the pressures that impinged on TVA both from the community at large and from powerful groups within. The outcome of the struggle among interest groups largely determined the fate of this great New Deal social experiment.

All the bodies of material listed above deal extensively with interest

Table 6.1 Theoretical background of the political model

Conflict theory	Community power theory	Interest group theory
1 Conflict and competition	1 Forms of power and influence	1 Influence of internal groups
2 Emphasis on change processes	2 Multiple centers of influence	2 Influence of external groups
3 Role of 'classes' and interest groups in promoting conflict and change	3 Interest groups and veto groups	3 Conflict and competition
	4 Goal setting as a prime object of study	4 Divergent values as source of conflict
4 Role of conflict in 'political' decision making	5 'Spheres of influence' and study of specific issues	5 Goal-setting activities
	6 Interaction of multiple types of influence	

groups and the importance of group processes in the determination of the goals of the entire organization. When interest group theory, conflict theory and community power theory are linked together they form the theoretical background to a political interpretation of university governance. Some of the major emphases of each strand are shown in Table 6.1.

An outline of the political model

[. . .]

When we look at the complex and dynamic processes that explode on the modern campus today, we see neither the rigid, formal aspects of bureaucracy nor the calm, consensus-directed elements of an academic collegium. On the contrary, if student riots cripple the campus, if professors form unions and strike, if administrators defend their traditional positions, and if external interest groups and irate governors invade the academic halls, all these acts must be seen as political. They emerge from the complex fragmented social structure of the university and its 'publics', drawing on the divergent concerns and life-styles of hundreds of miniature subcultures. These groups articulate their interests in many different ways, bringing pressure on the decision-making process from any number of angles and using power and force whenever it is available and necessary. Power and influence, once articulated, go through a complex process until policies are shaped, reshaped and forged out of the competing claims of multiple groups. All this is a dynamic process, a process clearly indicating that the university is best understood as a 'politicized' institution – above all else the Political University.

To get some of the flavor of the political nature of the university let us turn to one of the first interviews at New York University, which was with a dean who was undoubtedly one of its strongest men. Toward the end of the interview he made the following comments:

Dean: Do you have an organization chart? O.K. Well you can just throw it away. Forget it, those little boxes are practically useless. Look, if you really want to find out how this university is run you're going to have to understand the tensions, the strains, and the fights that go on between the people. You see, this is a political problem of jockeying between various schools, colleges, departments, and individuals for their place in the sun. Each school, group, and individual pressures for his own goals, and it's a tough counterplay of groups struggling for control. You've really got to understand the "politics" if you want to know how the place works.

Interviewer: Do you realize how often you've used the term "political" or "politics" in the last few minutes? Is that a deliberate choice of words?

Dean: I'll say it is – most deliberate. I think the imagery of politics is very helpful in understanding the operation of this place. Of course, this doesn't necessarily imply "dirty" politics. I simply mean that you've got to understand the political forces – both inside and outside – that are trying to control this place. There are pressures impinging on the officials of the university from all directions, and in a real sense the management of this university is a balancing process. It's a task of balancing the demands of various groups against each other and against the university's resources. People often call the university administrators "bureaucrats", implying that they are red-tape specialists, but that is a childishly naive understanding of our role. Sure, there are indeed some lower level administrators who are paper-pushers and bureaucrats in the old sense of the word, but the men in the critical roles are not bureaucrats, they are *politicians* struggling to make dreams come true and fighting to balance interest groups off against each other. This place is more like a political jungle, alive and screaming, than a rigid, quiet bureaucracy.[8]

This comment and dozens of similar observations suggested that a study of the political dynamics surrounding decision making would help unravel some of the difficulties in studying academic administration.

However, there simply was no available model in organization theory that could analyze these activities. Instead, it was necessary to build a primitive sort of 'political model', a framework for study that would provoke some insights into the nature of the political processes in organizations. This was no sophisticated model but instead a set of questions that could be used to get a hold on complex processes. Figure 6.1 illustrates the whole model as it was finally developed. [. . .]

A glance at Fig. 6.1 shows that the political model has several stages, all of which center around the policy-forming processes. We selected policy formation as the central focal point, for major policies commit the organization to definite goals, set the strategies for reaching those goals, and in general determine the long-range destiny of the organization. Policy decisions are not just any decisions, but instead are those that have major impact, those that mold the organization's future. In short, policies are the 'critical' decisions, not merely the 'routine' ones. Of course, in any practical situation it is often difficult to separate major policies from routine decisions, for issues that seem minor at one point may later prove to be decisive or vice versa. In general, however, policies are those decisions that bind the organization to important courses of action. Because policies are so important, people throughout the organization try to influence them in order to see that their special values are implemented. Policy becomes a major point of conflict, a watershed of partisan activity that permeates the life of the university. In light of its importance, policy becomes the center of the political analysis. Just as the political scientist often selects legislative acts in Congress as the focal point of his analysis of the state's political processes, we as organization theorists have selected policy decisions as the key to studying organizational conflict and change.

The sociologist wants to know how the social structure of the university influences the decision processes, how political pressures are brought on decision makers, how decisions are forged out of the conflict, and how the policies, once set, are implemented. Thus our political model points to five points of analysis: social structure features, interest articulation processes, legislative phases, policy outcomes and policy executions.[9] Let us look at each of these stages. Incidentally, it may be helpful for the reader to follow the discussion by continually referring back to Fig. 6.1.

First is a *social structure*, i.e. a configuration of social groups with basically different life-styles and political interests. The crucial point is that the differences often lead to conflict, for what is in the interest of one group may damage another. It is important, then, to examine the social setting with its fragmented groups, divergent goal aspiration, and conflicting claims on the decision makers. The university has a particularly complex pluralistic social system because many groups inside and outside the organization are pushing in various directions, according to their own special interests. One need only glance at the various outside 'publics' of a university to see its external social context, and the same glance turned inward would

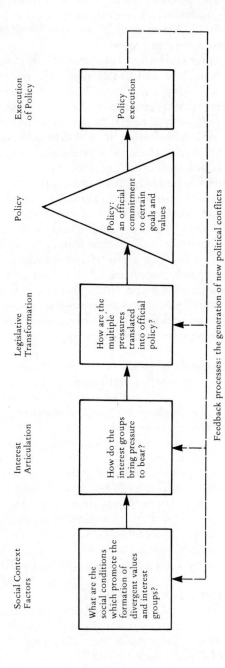

Social Context
Factors

Interest
Articulation

Legislative
Transformation

Policy

Execution
of Policy

What are the
social conditions
which promote the
formation of
divergent values
and interest
groups?

How do the
interest groups
bring pressure
to bear?

How are the
multiple
pressures
translated
into official
policy?

Policy:
an official
commitment
to certain
goals and
values

Policy
execution

Feedback processes: the generation of new political conflicts

Figure 6.1 A simple political model.

immediately reveal the internal social structure with its fragmented interest groups. Many of the current conflicts on the campus have their roots in the complexity of the academic social structure and in the complex goals and values held by these divergent groups.

Second is the process of *interest articulation*. Groups with conflicting values and goals must somehow translate them into effective influence if they are to obtain favorable action by legislative bodies. How does a powerful group exert its pressure, what threats or promises can it make, and how does it translate its desires into political capital? There are many forms of interest articulation at work among the policy makers from every quarter and it assumes a multitude of shapes. Political intervention comes from external groups, from faculty groups demanding authority, from rioting student groups, and from officials who apply their formal authority. In this political tangle the articulation of interests is a fundamental process.

Third is the dynamics by which articulated interests are translated into policies – the *legislative stage*. Legislative bodies respond to pressures, transforming the conflict into politically feasible policy. In the process, many claims are played off against one another, negotiations are undertaken, compromises are forged, and rewards are divided. Committees meet, commissions report, negotiators bargain, and powerful people 'higgle and haggle' about the eventual policy. Not only must we identify the types of interest groups and the methods they use to bring pressure but we must also clarify the translation process by which all these pressures are negotiated into a formal policy.

Fourth, the *formulation of policy* is the end result. The articulated interests have gone through conflict and compromise stages and the final legislative action is taken. The policy is the official climax to the conflict and represents an authoritative, binding decision to commit the organization to one set of possible alternative actions, to one set of goals and values.

Finally, the *execution of policy* occurs. The conflict comes to a climax, the battle is at least officially over, and the resulting policy is turned over to the bureaucrats for routine execution. Of course, this is oversimplified, but it is remarkable that yesterday's vicious battle may indeed become today's boring bureaucratic chore. This may not be the end of the matter, however, for two things are likely to happen. First, the major losers in the conflict may take up their arms again for a new round of interest articulation and, secondly, the execution of policy inevitably causes a *feedback cycle*, in which the policy generates new tensions, new vested interests, and a new cycle of political conflict.

In summary, the broad outline of the political system looks like this: a complex social structure generates multiple pressures, many forms of power and pressure impinge on the decision makers, a legislative stage translates these pressures into policy, and a policy execution phase finally generates feedback in the form of new conflicts.

[. . .]

Notes

1 Ralf Dahrendorf, *Class and Class Conflict in Industrial Society*. Stanford: Stanford University Press, 1959; Lewis Coser, *The Functions of Social Conflict*. Glencoe: Free Press, 1956; Lewis Coser, 'Social Conflict and the Theory of Social Change'. *British Journal of Sociology*, **8**, 197–209 (1957); William A. Gamson, *Power and Discontent*. Homewood, Ill.: Dorsey Press, 1968; Dorwin Cartwright, 'Influence, Leadership, Control'. *In* James G. March (ed.), *Handbook of Organizations*. Chicago: Rand McNally, 1956, pp. 1–47; William A. Gamson, 'Rancorous Conflict – Community Politics'. *American Sociological Review*, **31**, 71–81 (1966).

2 Floyd Hunter, *Community Power Structure*. Garden City, N.Y.: Anchor, 1963; Robert Dahl, *Who Governs?* New Haven: Yale University Press, 1961. For extensive reviews of the community power literature, see Nelson Polsby, *Community Power and Political Theory*. New Haven: Yale University Press, 1963, and John Walton, 'Discipline, Method and Community Power: A Note on the Sociology of Knowledge'. *American Sociological Review*, **31**(5), 684–9 (1966).

3 For example, see David B. Truman, *The Government Process*. New York: Alfred Knopf, 1951, and Robert Dahl, *Who Governs?* New Haven: Yale University Press, 1961. See also Earl Latham, *The Group Basis of Politics*. Ithica: Cornell University Press, 1952; V. O. Key Jr, *Politics, Parties and Pressure Groups*. New York: Crowell, 1958; and Arthur Bently, *The Process of Government*. Chicago: Chicago University Press, 1908.

4 Some of the prison studies most directly involved with this issue are as follows: D. R. Cressey and W. Krassowski, 'Inmate Organization and Anomie in American Prisons and Soviet Labor Camps'. *Social Problems*, **5**, 217–30 (1957); F. E. Hartung and M. Floch, 'A Social–Psychological Analysis of Prison Riots: An Hypothesis'. *Journal of Criminal Law and Criminology*, **47**, 51–7 (1956); R. H. McCleery, 'The Governmental Process and Informal Social Control'. *In* D. R. Cressey (ed.), *The Prison Studies in Institutional Organization and Change*. New York: Holt, Rinehart and Winston, 1961, pp. 149–88; L. R. Ephron, 'Group Conflicts in Organization: A Critical Appraisal of Recent Theories'. *Berkeley Journal of Sociology*, **6**, 56–72 (1961); G. M. Sykes, 'The Corruption of Authority and Rehabilitation'. *Social Forces*, **34**, 257–62 (1956); and H. P. Gouldner, 'Dimensions of Organization Commitment'. *Administrative Science Quarterly*, **4**, 469–90 (1960).

5 Fritz J. Roethlisberger and William J. Nickson, *Management and the Worker*. Cambridge, Mass.: Harvard University Press, 1939. For a more extensive review, see Peter Blau and Richard Scott, *Formal Organizations*. San Francisco: Chandler, 1962, ch. 4.

6 Melville Dalton, *Men Who Manage*. New York: Wiley, 1959; 'Conflicts between Staff and Line Managerial Officers'. *American Sociological Review*, **15**, 342–51 (1950); 'Unofficial Union–Management Relations'. *American Sociological Review*, **15**, 611–19 (1950).

7 Phillip Selznick, *TVA and the Grass Roots*, Berkeley: University of California Press, 1949.

8 Interview No. 14, p. 3.

9 The following discussion depends partly on Gabriel Almond and James Coleman, *The Politics of Developing Areas*. Princeton: Princeton University Press, 1960, ch. 1. The categories and stages, however, do not directly follow their research.

7

The micropolitics of schools

Eric Hoyle

Committee member: You didn't get your own way today, Alec!
Chief Education Officer: You haven't read the minutes yet!

Apocryphal

There is an organizational underworld, the world of micropolitics, which has received only limited attention from theorists and researchers. It finds little place in organization theory and even less in management theory. It is rarely discussed in any formal context within organizations and it finds virtually no place in the teaching of educational administration. It is almost a taboo subject in 'serious' discussion, yet informally it is a favourite theme of organizational gossip as people talk about 'playing politics', 'hidden agendas', 'organizational mafias', 'Machiavellianism', and so forth. When this aspect of organizational life *is* mooted, for example, on teachers' courses, there is a *frisson* of recognition and although course members have many tales to tell of micropolitical skulduggery, they prefer to tell them in the bar rather than submit them to analysis in the serious context of a course discussion. [. . .]

Thus the micropolitical aspects of organizations are widely recognized. 'We all know that it goes on' but just what 'it' is remains vague. 'It' also generates a considerable degree of ambivalence as if we did not wish to concede that organizational and administrative processes are anything less than rational.

The domain of micropolitics

Micropolitics can be said to consist of the strategies by which individuals and groups in organizational contexts seek to use their resources of authority and influence to further their interests (Hoyle, 1982). It might be argued that this is simply a definition of management, but, although a clear distinction between management and micropolitics cannot be drawn, it is worthwhile making a rough and ready distinction in order to bring micropolitics into focus. [. . .]

Micropolitics is best perceived as a continuum, one end of which is virtually indistinguishable from conventional management procedures but from which it diverges on a number of dimensions – interests, interest sets, power, strategies and legitimacy – to the point where it constitutes almost a separate organizational world of illegitimate, self-interested manipulation. One can only speculate on the interaction between management and micropolitics. It may well be that micropolitics is shaped by the formal structures and procedures of an organization. Perhaps these give the organization a 'dominant' character with micropolitics 'recessive' and limited in scope to the interstices. An image would be the frame of a Georgian window representing the organizational 'structure' and the glass representing the micropolitics. But what is the 'significant' component of a window: the frame or the glass? They are, of course, integral. On the other hand, it could well be that the 'real' life of the organization is the micropolitical, with the structure either an inert concept ritualistically treated as the determinant of organizational behaviour but in fact having little real influence, or as only given its life by the operation of micropolitics. In practice, the relationship between management and micropolitics will be variable both between kinds of organization and between organizations of the same kind. [. . .]

The essence of micropolitics, and the characteristics which most clearly distinguish this domain from management, are the *strategies* employed. Management, too, involves a variety of procedures which can be termed strategies and which are coterminous with micropolitics at one end of our continuum, but thence a divergence occurs. Bargaining, for example, is both a managerial and micropolitical strategy. In industrial organizations, bargaining between management and unions is an integral part of the administrative process. However, bargaining becomes more micropolitical to the degree that it is implicit rather than explicit, outside rather than inside formal structures and procedures, and draws on informal resources of influence. The difficulty is, of course, that while formal bargaining is occurring at the management level, there might well be a hidden micropolitical agenda of which all parties are aware and which shapes the formal procedures. As one moves away from this end of the dimension, strategies become more detached from the formal procedures. [. . .] Handy (1976) discusses such strategies as the distortion of information, the imposition of rules and procedures, and the control of rewards. It should be noted that those organizational members who have managerial power will also enjoy the greatest access to micropolitical strategies. Thus the head, who has a high degree of authority and can exert a considerable degree of control over organizational activities, will also have at his disposal a wide range of micropolitical strategies.

Strategies are deployed in pursuit of individual or group *interests*. Again some interests are an essential part of the administrative process. These can be referred to as 'professional' interests and centre on commitments to a particular curriculum, syllabus, mode of pupil grouping, teaching method, etc. It would be unusual for the staff of a school to be in total agreement on these matters, but where conflicts occur there are formal means for resolving these. Professional interests become part of the micropolitical process according to the strategies used to further them. Personal interests focus on such issues as status, promotion and working conditions. These interests, too, can be pursued via administrative procedures but are perhaps more likely to be pursued via micropolitical strategies, as they are matters which tend not to be openly discussed. A difficult empirical problem is to distinguish professional from personal interests, because the latter are often presented as the former, as interpretations of the interests of pupils. Thus a demand for increased time for one's subject is presented in terms of its importance to pupils, whereas the real interest of the teacher is in personal aggrandisement and empire building. Or a teacher's resistance to a particular innovation may be presented in professional terms as not being in the best educational interests of pupils, whereas this may conceal the teacher's personal interest which is to avoid the need to acquire new skills or otherwise upset established routine or even a genuine fear of the unknown (see Marland, 1982).

Interests are pursued by *interest sets*. This term is preferred to *interest groups* because the latter term conveys a greater cohesion and permanence than might be the case. Interest sets will be coterminous with units such as the management team. However, less formal interest sets might emerge. Some of these may have formal membership and administrative status, e.g. teacher unions. Other sets may mobilize on the basis of age: the 'old guard' versus the 'young Turks'. Others may mobilize on the basis of attitudes to change; Burns (1955) distinguished between *cliques* who were committed to the status quo and *cabals* which were committed to organizational change. Yet other sets may mobilize when specific issues are to the fore. Thus women staff members may constitute an interest set in resisting the expectation that they will act as cooks and washers-up when social events are organized. Still other sets may be based on external friendship groups, based perhaps on common membership of drama societies, choirs, golf clubs, churches, etc., and provide general support for each other on a range of issues. Of course, membership of interest sets will be overlapping and, in matters concerned with school policy, there is the likelihood that interest sets may combine as a coalition, an aspect of micropolitics studied by Selznick (1957) and Bacharach and Lawler (1980) among others.

The fourth component of the domain of micropolitics is *power*. [. . .] At the 'management' end of our hypothetical continuum the power will be exercised in the form of authority, but as one moves along to the domain of micropolitics, influence will be the dominant mode.

Thus, although it is not possible to draw any hard and fast distinction between administration and micropolitics, because they can be virtually coterminous at one end of our hypothesized continuum, micropolitics is more likely to be orientated to *interests* rather than *goals*, *coalitions* rather than *departments*, *influence* rather than *authority*, *strategies* rather than *procedures*.

Some approaches to the study of micropolitics

Micropolitics is not well established as a field of enquiry. Some of the reasons for this will be obvious from the preceding discussion. There is no clear distinction between the study of organizations, management and micropolitics, and a number of organizational theorists deal with this aspect of organizations. Micropolitics is a proper subject of a variety of disciplines – social psychology, anthropology, sociology, politics and economics – but hitherto no interdisciplinary approach has emerged, nor have the different disciplinary approaches taken much cognisance of each other. A third problem turns on the question of legitimacy. Approaches to micropolitics tend to assume legitimacy and focus on those aspects which are a normal part of management processes, thus neglecting the important nonlegitimate aspects of the domain. Finally, in so far as theories have to be tested via empirical studies of some kind, micropolitics will be neglected because the area is so sensitive that data is difficult to obtain – it is clearly tautologous to say that micropolitics is a politically sensitive area. Nevertheless, in spite of these problems, it is perhaps worthwhile to indicate the kinds of approaches which bear on the study of this domain.

Exchange theory has a far broader application in the social sciences than to micropolitics alone, but it is perhaps the most general of social science perspectives which can be applied to the domain. Homans (1961) has developed an exchange theory based on an economic calculus of benefits, which, reduced to a catchphrase, can be expressed as 'You scratch my back, and I'll scratch yours.' Thus A does something for B which has its *costs* in terms of some species of resource. Similarly, B does something for A in return, which generates costs for B. Both gain from this exchange, that is they both experience *rewards*. When these rewards exceed in some way the costs incurred, the outcome will be *profit*. Homans (1958) erects a micro-economic social theory on this notion of exchange which need not be elaborated here except to note that he makes the functionalist assumption that there is a 'free market' on the exchange of goods and services and that where an exchange relationship is entered into both participants will profit. However, the 'goods' which are traded in these exchanges are unequal and the profits unequal, or one participant may experience a loss. Thus a head has a greater range of resources and can make a teacher – explicitly or implicitly – 'an offer he can't refuse', whereby the 'profit' of the head is greater than that of a teacher.' [. . .]

Blau's (1964) theory of exchange in social life differs from that of others in two important ways. One is that it takes more account than other studies of the effects of differential power in social interaction. The other is that it transcends the microsociological level and concerns itself with the *structures* which are operated by the interplay of power and exchange. Blau is not as optimistic as Homans about the attainment of an equilibrium which is equally satisfying to both parties. There are unbalanced exchanges which have their costs as well as their benefits, and behaviour may be as much concerned with minimizing unpleasantness as maximizing pleasantness. [. . .]

Exchange is not simply an unproblematic mutual backscratching activity. In many organizations the exchange is formalized and governed by explicit procedures. These are the focus of theories of *bargaining*. Clearly such theories are more applicable to organizational contexts in which management and unions bargain, or where different units within the organization bargain with each other over, for example, the distribution of resources. Bargaining in schools is less explicit but does occur. There are a number of approaches to bargaining, but because we are here concerned only with illustrating approaches rather than undertaking a critical analysis of the full array, we can take as an example of an approach in this genre the work of Abell (1975):

> Essentially, then, a bargaining zone comprises a group of individuals (perhaps representing organisations not groups, i.e. other bargaining zones), normatively constrained, but with differing objectives, attempting to arrive at collective decisions through a complex process of influence and bargaining?

A bargaining zone consists of a set of actors, a set of decisions, an assumption that each actor has a clearly defined preferred outcome, an assumption that each actor attaches a clearly defined salience to each decision, i.e. how important he feels it necessary to exert influence, of the outcome. The bargaining zone is 'normatively constrained' because there are broad limitations in what is possible as an outcome. There will also be allocation norms which dictate why the particular set of decisions which fall within the zone do so. Abell depicts the bargaining process as occurring in two phases. The first is the *influence* phase, whereby members of the bargaining zone seek to change others' preferred outcomes. Thus A will agree to support B on some issue which is not particularly salient for A in exchange for B supporting A over an issue which is salient to B. This is followed by the *bargaining phase*, where actors bargain from their 'influenced' position to a collective decision. Bacharach and Lawler (1981) have developed a set of formal propositions related to bargaining which are based on the interplay betwen power and tactics which, although the examples are based on employer–union bargaining, have their analogies in the less formal contexts of day-to-day exchanges between heads and teachers.

[. . .]

The bargaining approach merges with what one might call *formal theories of organizational politics.* Perhaps the systematic theory of this genre is that developed by Bacharach and Lawler (1980). They summarize their approach to organizational politics as follows:

> An understanding of organisational politics requires an analysis of power, coalitions and bargaining. The power relationship is the context for political action and encompasses the most basic issues underlying organisational politics. As the primary mechanism through which individuals and subgroups acquire, maintain, and use power, coalitions crystallise and bring to the foreground the conflicting interests of organisational subgroups. Through bargaining, distinct coalitions attempt to achieve their political objectives and protect themselves from encroachments by opposing coalitions. Power, coalitions, and bargaining, therefore, constitute the three basic themes in our theoretical treatise on organisational politics.

Micropolitics in schools

[. . .]

The loosely coupled characteristic of the schools is likely to be a factor determining the amount of micropolitics. The problem for heads is that they have a high degree of authority but the legal sanctions which underpin this authority will only be invoked relatively infrequently. Moreover, teachers have a relatively high degree of autonomy supported by professional norms which inhibit the exercise of the legally based authority of the head. Thus the head's administrative control must depend to a considerable degree on the exercise of latent power and influence. This would seem to be likely to encourage the head's deployment of micropolitical strategies in the somewhat gaping interstices within the management structure. I have argued elsewhere (Hoyle, 1982) that the movement towards greater teacher participation in school policy, without any change in the head's ultimate responsibility for the internal activities of the school, may have led heads to have greater recourse to micropolitics in an attempt to fulfil this responsibility in the face of staff pressures towards policies which they cannot wholly support. On the teachers' side, micropolitical activity is probably inhibited to the degree that their preoccupations are with their classroom activities rather than school policy. However, in so far as they are involved in policy making they will have interests – personal, professional and perhaps macropolitical – and may well engage in micropolitics to further these.

For the teacher the stakes involved in micropolitical activity are relatively low compared with those which one might assume to be the case in industrial and commercial organizations. The potential rewards involved, as we will see below, will cluster around the issues of promotion and the quality of the work situation: what is to be taught to whom, when, where and how. One might therefore anticipate teachers' micropolitical activity to be devoted at least as much to protecting work conditions as to furthering educational policies. But it must be noted that although the stakes do not appear to be high, promotion does become a quite salient interest at certain points of many teachers' careers. It should be further noted that although the stakes of protecting one's work satisfaction may not appear to be high, it must be remembered that *relative deprivation* is keenly experienced and likely to motivate teachers to engage in micropolitical activity to redress circumstances which lead to such feelings (Hoyle, 1969).

As noted in the previous section, the sociological theory which appears to be most relevant to micropolitics is *exchange theory*, although it is worth reporting that the major protagonists see this as a theory which has general applicability to social behaviour and not simply to its more manipulative manifestations. Exchange theory is predicated on the existence of 'goods' and elsewhere I have attempted to classify the kinds of 'good' which might be involved in an exchange between heads and teachers (Hoyle, 1981):

The head has the following categories of "goods" available for exchange:

Material resources The head has a high degree of control over such resources as books and equipment which he can distribute differentially as part of the exchange process. It is perhaps significant that head-teachers tend not to democratise decisions over such allocations.

Promotion British headteachers have a greater direct control over promotion than their equivalent elsewhere. Their freedom to distribute scale-posts within their schools is a powerful resource which may not be brought out openly in a bargaining situation but is no less potent for remaining implicit. Heads also have a crucial role in the promotion of members of a staff to higher statuses in other schools since their references will be a key factor.

Esteem Heads are in a position to increase, or otherwise, the teacher's self-esteem and esteem in the eyes of colleagues through favourable remarks made privately or publicly.

Autonomy Heads are in a position to determine the degree of auton-omy enjoyed by teachers by refraining from monitoring their teaching and other activities.

Lax application of rules This resource is somewhat related to auton-omy. Heads are in a position to insist on rules being kept to the letter, but as an implicit bargaining ploy they may be willing 'to turn a blind eye' when rules are infringed. They can apply the rules differentially insisting on their observation in the case of teachers they have little regard for, but failing to do so in the case of teachers for whom they have a high regard or whose support they are seeking.

There is an imbalance between the bargaining resources of heads and teachers. The latter have fewer "goods" to trade and those that they have tend to be symbolic rather than material. Nevertheless, these are important to heads and some examples are:

Esteem The private or public expression of regard for the head as a person and as a professional.

Support The acceptance of the head's aims for the school.

Opinion leadership This is related to support and involves the use of personal influence in the staff group to gain acceptance for the head's goals or authority.

Conformity The acceptance of the rules and procedures laid down by the head. There may be a paradox here whereby the head is lax in the application of rules in those cases where the teachers are most willing to follow them.

Reputation The enhancement of the prestige of the school (and hence of the head) through examination success, sporting success, involvement in community activities, etc.

Thus, although the simple model of managerial authority depicts a head with considerable power over a group of necessarily compliant teachers, the reality is much more complex with implicit bargaining on the basis of different sets of "goods" shaping the relationship.

The important and difficult question is how the deal involved in an exchange is struck. Some deals will be the subject of explicit bargaining between a head and a group of teachers – perhaps a formal group such as an academic department, perhaps an informal group of teachers who are challenging a proposed policy change. In this instance the theories of bargaining such as those developed by Abell (1975) and others will apply. But although such explicit bargaining activity is a daily occurrence in industrial and commercial organizations, one's hunch is that it occurs less frequently in schools because it is contrary to the professional norms which pervade education. One might hypothesize that the 'deal' is signalled in highly subtle and informal ways, by language, gesture, symbolic action, and so forth. It can be approached only through an interpretive sociology or social psychology requiring the immersion of the investigator in the staff culture of the school. Of course, there is no guarantee that an investigator would make a correct interpretation because presumably those who might be involved in an exchange could misread or miss entirely the message.

A hypothetical example of an exchange between a primary school head and a teacher where the message is transmitted and received would be the following:

	Thoughts	*Speech*
Head:	This LEA request for a review of the maths curriculum is a nuisance. I can't find the time to do it. I wonder if I can con Jim Smith into taking it on? He has aspirations for a Scale III post.	Hello, Jim. How's Mary? Good. No, things aren't too bad but the office is never off my back these days. Look what I've had this morning; a request for a review of the maths syllabus. Maths is more in your line than mine isn't it?
Smith:	What's he up to? Is he hinting that I ought to take it on? I don't want extra work, especially discussing a syllabus with the rest of them, but it wouldn't do my promotion chances any harm. However, I had better not ask for it. That would be too risky.	Yes, it is really. That in-service course which you arranged for me to go on was useful. It shouldn't be too hard a job reviewing the maths syllabus in this school.
Head:	He seems to have bitten, so I'll come right out with it.	Yes, I remember that course. Is this review something that you'd be willing to take on? I'd be very grateful.
Smith:	I'll take it on, but how do I convey that I have expectations of promotion?	Yes, I don't mind taking it on. It's something which interests me and it will give me a chance to bring some of our colleagues in. And in any case, it will be good experience for me.
Head:	It's clear what he's after. How do I acknowledge that I recognise it as a bid for promotion?	Oh good. That's very helpful. Yes, the experience could turn out to be valuable.

This kind of two-person exchange is the simplest form of exchange relationship. There will be many such in the school, especially between the head and members of his staff. However, although exchanges may be limited to the interests of only the two people involved, schools are characterized by a network of exchange relationships which constitute a structure perhaps as potent with regard to the organizational character of the school as the formal authority structure. The interests which this system of exchange is designed to further will include personal and professional interests and those where these two types of interest are inseparable in practice. This exchange system will be relatively stable. Patterns will be established which, perhaps to a large extent, depend on the head's leadership style.

[. . .]

Some basic micropolitical strategies

We have no map of the territory of micropolitics. However, the following are some of the more obvious strategies.

Dividing and ruling

This is a political strategy of long ancestry and we may assume that it is an element in the micropolitics of the school. In fact, the school is likely to be particularly prone to this strategy of control on the part of the headteacher because of its structural looseness. There are perhaps two variants of this strategy. One is for the head to avoid full meetings of staff or to call them only as meetings-for-report and to strike separate deals on, say, capitation matters, with individual teachers or departments. Negotiations are easier to handle in a less formal setting than a meeting and this approach avoids comparisons being made between the separate individuals and units until the decision is *fait accompli* and the overall outcome is known, if at all. A challenge would inevitably generate conflict, which teachers generally prefer to avoid, or involve the less favoured individuals or groups appearing to be seeking to take something away from the more favoured. There are some schools, for example, in which the number of available scale-posts and their actual distribution is unknown to the staff as a whole.

The other use of this strategy is to have matters discussed by a full staff meeting with, in the instances where scarce resources are to be disproportionately distributed among the parts of the school, the head insisting on taking the role of 'honest broker' and intervening only to resolve disputes between individuals or groups, thus retaining his power to determine events without appearing to be the *fons et origo* of unequal treatment.

Co-optation

This entails the involvement of those whose support the head seeks or whose potential opposition has to be diverted. Co-optation is a well-documented strategy in organizational politics, but the question of how it functions *symbolically* is unclear. [. . .] Co-optation may well cover the entire continuum. At one end is the head's genuine desire to have the voice of some particular individual or group heard in the decision-making process. At the other end would be *tokenism*, the involvement of, say, a young teacher or a woman teacher simply as a symbol designed to quieten opposition. The effectiveness of co-optation will depend upon the interpretations of members of staff which may range from a positive response to the co-optation as an indication that a particular 'voice' is to be heard, through to the position where the co-optation is recognized as symbolic but, as such, a genuine sensitivity to certain 'voices' and a worthy 'symbolic question' through to an interpretation of tokenism as an agreed attempt at manipulation.

Displacement

Teachers sometimes emerge from staff meetings saying: 'What was all that about?' This question suggests that micropolitical activity had been going on but the precise nature of the conflict of interests had not been obvious to those teachers who were neither directly involved nor had interpreted the messages. The 'real' issue had been 'displaced' with the debate centring on a proxy issue. The reason for displacement is clearly to conceal these 'real' interests which might be considered to be professionally unworthy. Thus the strategy is to gain support for the proxy issue. [. . .]

Bennett and Wilkie (1973) describe a conflict between the head of art and the head of science in a Scottish comprehensive school, ostensibly over the professional issue of how wide a choice over their options pupils should have, but in reality the issues in the dispute were about status and power. This was no doubt a correct interpretation of motive made by Bennett and Wilkie as experienced observers of school management. However, the difficulties in interpretation are obvious, because in such disputes the balance between the 'personal' and 'professional' motives is perhaps not wholly clear to the protagonists themselves.

Controlling information

How information is acquired, distributed, presented, doctored or withheld is micropolitical. Information may be a 'good' to be exchanged and therefore be an element in exchange theory. But information is also a means of non-negotiable control. It is a powerful weapon in the armoury of headteachers who have access to different kinds of information such as what one might call *policy-related* knowledge, e.g. official reports, LEA policy statements, comparative statistical data (e.g. on exam results); *political systems knowledge*, e.g. emerging LEA policies, the concerns of LEA inspectors, the views of governors, etc.; and *school-related knowledge*, e.g. finances, resources, Burnham points totals, etc. This information is amenable to the various 'treatments' suggested above and these constitute a powerful resource for the head. It is unlikely that individual teachers, or sets of teachers, have access to the same amount of information as the head. Nevertheless, a micropolitical strategy on the part of teachers is the deployment of such information as they can acquire. [. . .]

Controlling meetings

Meetings are perhaps less significant political arenas in schools than in other forms of organization. In primary schools the full staff meeting, held with variable frequency and formality, constitutes the only such arena. In secondary schools the structures, frequency and formality of meetings are more complex. [. . .]

We know little about the functions, especially the micropolitical functions, of meetings in schools, although they certainly have symbolic functions other than those for which they are overtly called. Bailey (1977) makes a distinction between two kinds of committees in universities:

> Some committees offer the opportunity either to shape or to show off an attitude: their proceedings are marked by ceremonial and formality and posturing to an extent which suggests that the exhibition has an intrinsic value and is not being directed towards getting something done. Along with the ceremonial style goes a concern with policy and principle and a tendency to avoid the discussion of persons.
>
> The committees which show the opposite characteristics, being unceremonious, informal, intolerant of expressive posturing, and ready to talk about persons-in-the-round, have the following features: the members think that what they are doing is of practical (not symbolic) importance; the committee is not large; it has a continuing existence; the members are not delegates from outside interests but answer only to their consciences; their proceedings are private and the members are relatively homogeneous in status. Attitude-shaping and expressive behaviour generally are inappropriate, firstly because the members already know one another's attitudes, and secondly because there is a tacit agreement on values, or (which comes to the same thing) an unquestioning acceptance of the book of rules.

It is interesting to speculate on the prevalence of these forms of committee, or the mixture of the two sets of characteristics in schools. The second type of committee identified by Bailey would normally be a committee of a small number of members of staff meeting regularly and coming to share the same values. In schools, the likely contender for this form is the management team. Full staff meetings in large secondary schools are perhaps more likely to adopt the latter form. In primary schools, the full staff meeting would be the only form of committee. One does not have the evidence to say what form staff meetings generally take in primary schools as it is likely to vary according to the head's leadership style. One can hypothesize that the formal committees are, perhaps paradoxically, those in which manipulative micropolitics are most in play. In the smaller 'community' committees, shared assumptions make manipulation both obvious and inappropriate; the mode will be one of exchange, the 'bargain' being implicit but generally understood. In the more 'organizational' meeting conflict will be more explicit but formalized. But because it is more formalized, and because the head cannot guarantee to achieve agreement on an informal 'exchange' basis, he or she is more likely to engage in manipulative micropolitics both before and during the meeting. The following are hypothetical examples of how a head might seek to ensure that a staff meeting arrives at a 'preferred' outcome (Hoyle, 1981):

1 *'Rigging' agendas*. The head controls the agenda, thus 'difficult' items can be kept off, worded as a routine piece of business, conflated with less tendentious items or placed low in the order of the agenda.

2 *'Losing' recommendations*. We can here envisage a situation in which a head has established a working party to consider a particular issue but does not approve of its eventual recommendations. The strategy would involve referring these recommendations to sets of other committees in the hope that they would go trekking around the consultative system until some group opposed them or until interest waned and the recommendations became inert.

3 *'Nobbling' members*. We can again envisage a situation where an item about which the head has strong views *has* made the agenda of a staff meeting. If the head is aware that a group of teachers, perhaps a working party which has been successful in having its recommendations up for consideration, is committed to an opposite viewpoint from that of the head, the latter may make pre-emptive moves to counter this by mobilizing support among uncommitted teachers. This would be achieved through casual corridor conversations. At the end of an innocuous conversation the 'nobbling' process might occur as follows:

Head: Oh, by the way. Have you seen that the issue of the ten-day timetable is on the agenda for the staff meeting?
Teacher: Yes. I heard that it was coming up.
Head: Apparently Mr Saltro's group is recommending it strongly.
Teacher: So I'd heard.
Head: I think it would lead to problems. Don't you?
Teacher: Well, I hadn't thought about it much.
Head: Don't you think it would cause a lot of unnecessary confusion amongst the pupils?
Teacher: I suppose it would.
Head: So you agree that that is the danger?
Teacher: Now that I think about it, I suppose I do.
Head: Fine. I'm glad there will be someone other than myself pointing this out at the meeting. I take it that you'll make your views known?
Teacher: Well, I'm not one for speaking much at meetings but I suppose if there's discussion I'll probably say something.
Head: Good.

[. . .]

4 *Invoking outside bodies.* The head is the one person on the staff to interact with a wide range of bodies whose activities impinge on the school. This puts the head in a strong position to advance a particular policy, or to stymie one, on the basis of the alleged views of these outside bodies:

> The LEA wouldn't provide the money.
> The governors seem to want it.
> The parents seem to be keen on it.
> I gather the Chief Adviser is strongly against it.

5 *'Interpreting' consensus.* Here one envisages a situation in which there has been a discussion in which relatively few staff members have spoken on some recommendation of the head and these have been roughly divided into pros and cons. At some point the head says: 'Well then, we all seem to be agreed.' The staff are fully aware that no such consensus exists but for a combination of reasons – out of deference, for 'exchange' reasons, or because of the norms which inhibit the call for a vote – the head's interpretation goes unchallenged.

6 *'Massaging' minutes.* If the head has chaired the meeting then the responsibility for the minutes is his and he can ensure that they are worded so as to best represent the head's own views.

[. . .]

Conclusion

The existence of micropolitics is widely recognized. However, there is a conceptual problem involved in distinguishing between the formal procedures of bargaining and negotiation which are part and parcel of normal management activity and the less formal strategies which interest sets utilize in pursuit of their interests. The study of organizational micropolitics is still very much underdeveloped and currently a number of perspectives are being brought to bear on this aspect of organizational behaviour.

Schools are perhaps particularly prone to micropolitical activity for two main reasons. One is their loosely coupled characteristic which yield the 'spaces' in which such activity can flourish. The second is the competing forms of legitimacy in decision making which arise because the formal legitimacy of the head is challenged by alternative professional and democratic forms which are held to be particularly appropriate to schools. This leaves heads with the problem of balancing their responsibility against the expectations of collegiality.

The head has relatively few tangible rewards to induce teachers to work for the school as a collective, the main reward being promotion, or support for promotion, which is perhaps currently of declining value in the context of falling rolls. There is thus a premium on symbolic rewards of various kinds. Exchange theory is perhaps one of the most important theoretical perspectives on micropolitics in schools. However, in schools as well as larger society, exchange is not necessarily a self-adjusting market and the unequal distribution of power must figure in any analysis of micropolitics. The power-play of the formal bargaining which occurs in industrial organizations is not greatly in evidence in schools and one must look to the manipulative exercise of power through the use of micropolitical strategies in order to understand fully what is happening in schools.

[. . .]

References

Abell, P. (ed.) (1975). *Organizations as Bargaining and Influence Systems*. London: Heinemann.
Bacharach, S. B. and Lawler, E. J. (1980). *Power and Politics in Organizations*. San Francisco: Jossey-Bass.
Bacharach, S. B. and Lawler, E. J. (1981). *Bargaining: Power, Tactics and Outcomes*. San Francisco: Jossey-Bass.
Bailey, F. G. (1977). *Morality and Expediency: The Folklore of Academic Politics*. Oxford: Blackwell.
Bennett, S. and Wilkie, R. (1973). 'Structural conflict in school organization'. *In* Fowler, G., Morris, V. and Ozga, J. (eds), *Decision-Making in Educational Administration*. London: Heinemann.
Blau, P. M. (1964). *Exchange and Power in Social Life*. New York: Wiley.
Burns, T. (1955). 'The reference of conduct in small groups'. *Human Relations*, **8**.
Handy, C. B. (1976). *Understanding Organizations*. Harmondsworth: Penguin.
Homans, G. C. (1958). 'Human behaviour as exchange'. *American Journal of Sociology*, **63**(6).
Homans, G. C. (1961). *Social Behaviour: Its Elementary Forms*. London: Routledge and Kegan Paul.
Hoyle, E. (1969). 'Professional stratification and anomie in the teaching profession'. Pedagogica Europaea Vol. 5, *The Changing Role of the Professional Educator*. Elsevier: Amsterdam.
Hoyle, E. (1981). 'The process of management'. *In Management and the School*, E 323, Block 3. Milton Keynes: Open University Press.
Hoyle, E. (1982). 'Micropolitics of educational organizations'. *Educational Management and Administration*, **10**(2).
Marland, M. (1982). 'The politics of improvement in schools'. *Educational Management and Administration*, **10**(2).
Selznick, P. (1957). *Leadership in Administration*. New York: Harper and Row.

8

Organizations as social inventions: Rethinking assumptions about change

T. Barr Greenfield

Organizations serve as common targets for critics and reformers who see social institutions as frequently (if not inherently) opposed to human purposes and needs (Ash, 1971; Katz, 1971). Consequently, change agents with varied but intense visions for improving organizations seek to transform them in ways that will liberate rather than frustrate and alienate the human spirit (see Argyris, 1964; Bennis, 1966; Miles, 1965; Rothman, 1972).

Two critical assumptions appear to underlie this view of organizations. One is that organizations exist apart from people, thus making it possible to modify organizations or to design new ones without changing people. The second is that the goals of an organization are independent of those held by individuals within it. If these assumptions are accepted, a line of reasoning emerges which holds that the way to improve organizations is to redesign and direct them towards humane goals. The strategy for organizational improvement thus derived demands the shaping of organizations in terms of human needs rather than organizational requirements. Although there is dispute about what to change within the organization, there is usually agreement that organizations are entities capable of improvement and that organizations and individuals have goals which would be better achieved if the organizations were smaller, less bureaucratic, 'healthier', more structured, or more *something*, which would change their internal structure or processes.

In contrast, this chapter argues that most of our current strategies for changing organizations rest upon an oversimplification that conveniently separates people and organizations. If we see individuals and organizations as inextricably intertwined, it may not be so easy to alter organizations without also cutting into something unexpectedly human. It is surely desirable that we have a vision of how organizations might be better; but we should also understand what we are changing when we offer new models for life in organizations. Such an understanding takes us back to some curious and usually neglected phenomena found in the way people see the world – particularly in the way we come to hold or change our views. In these times, when many social institutions are under attack for changing or for failing to change, it is appropriate to ask just what it is we change when we change an organization.

Within the general problem of what we mean by the concept 'organization', I wish to raise two specific questions: 'What is an organization that it can have such a thing as a goal?', and 'How do the goals of individuals bear upon those of the organization – if, indeed, it is appropriate to speak of organizational goals?' These questions are clearly interrelated; they may be, in fact, merely different ways of asking whether an organization is something more than the sum of its parts. These are not new questions in organizational analysis, and I do not propose new answers. I do want to suggest that we seldom ask these questions or seek a compelling set of answers when we engage in efforts at organizational change. Such indifference cannot really be justified; adequate answers to these questions raise some serious doubts about our ability to change organizations or to design them to meet human needs.

What is an organization that it can have a goal?

At a pragmatic level, we have no difficulty believing that organizations are real and that they have goals apart from those of specific individuals within them. Prisons, banks, schools, hospitals, political parties and armies are organizations whose reality and whose goals the individual may deny only to his disadvantage or even at his peril. That these organizations are 'real' and that they have different goals seem obvious. Theorists substantiate this common-sense view of organizations by usually dealing with organizations as objective 'facts' (see e.g. Mouzelis, 1967: Parsons, 1958). Where there are differences among theorists, the argument usually turns on the nature of the particular 'fact' observed, not upon what predisposes us to see organizations in terms of one set of facts rather than another. Most theoretical perspectives on organizations foster our view of them as powerful, goal-oriented entities that operate *on* people rather than through them. A look at two major conceptions of organizations – systems theory and bureaucratic theory – reinforces this conclusion.

Bureaucratic theories of organization locate reality in structure, which, as expressed through specialization and hierarchy, operates to achieve pre-determined goals. In this view, organizations 'planfully' solve problems, they 'drive toward rationality', and they 'invade' realms of action traditionally controlled by individuals (Gouldner, 1959, p. 418). Thus the organization in effect strips its members of their personal motives and replaces them with those that serve the purposes of the organization. Accepting this view of the power of organizations apart from people within them, Perrow (1970, p. 4) argues that '. . . people's attitudes are shaped at least as much by the organization in which they work as by their pre-existing attitudes'. And again from Perrow:

> . . . a great deal of organizational effort is exerted to *control* the effects of extra-organizational influences upon personnel. Daily, people come contaminated into the organization. . . . Many of the irritating aspects of organizational structure are designed to control these sources of contamination (1970, p. 52).

In contrast to the bureaucratic view of organizations, the systems perspective rejects the notion of the organization as striving to achieve goals external to itself, but retains the concept of organization as an entity apart from its members and with power over them. An open system is defined as:

> . . . a bounded collection of interdependent parts . . . maintained in a steady state in relation to each other and the environment by means of (1) standard modes of operation, and (2) feedback from the environment about the consequences of system actions (Miles, 1965, p. 15).

Thus systems theorists see homeostasis and feedback as critical in organizational life, because these processes operate to give purpose to the functioning organization. In the systems view, organizations do not appear as mechanisms designed for the single-minded pursuit of goals set by external hands; rather, organizations discover goals through their capacity to respond and adapt to their environments. Therefore, a fundamental problem for organizations is the discovery of goals that will maintain the integrity of the system and ensure its survival in the environment. On this account, the 'operative' goals (Perrow, 1961) of organizations, as distinct from those formally promulgated for them, are obscure and hard to identify. For this reason, systems theorists are usually not concerned with specific goals of organizations, but only with the quality of basic organizational processes – with the health of the organization.

The idea of an organization's responding like an organism to its environment and thus discovering an equilibrium or goal which enables it to survive in its environment is a recurrent theme among systems theorists (see e.g. Etzioni, 1960; Katz and Kahn, 1966; Merton, 1957; Selznick, 1948; Thompson and McEwen, 1958). Of course there are critics of bureaucratic and systems theory who proceed from a psychological viewpoint designed to take the individual into account. However, even these critics are apt to see the organization as a thing apart from its members. Thus Argyris (1964, pp. 197–220) advocates that organization structure be redesigned to meet human needs – especially higher-level needs like self-actualization. Bennis (1968) recommends that organizations learn to change quickly so they can adapt to complex, turbulent environments. According to this view, organizations that cannot learn to change, and change quickly, will suffer the penalty of any ill-adapted organism, i.e. extinction. This evolution will leave us with small, quick-witted, democratic organizations, in contrast to the ponderous bureaucratic forms now expiring around us.

The point I wish to emphasize is that these views of organizations and these beliefs about what should be done to deal with their 'problems' all imply a single, goal-oriented entity that *is* the organization: they assume this entity works (perhaps badly or dysfunctionally) to impose pattern on its members. Thus, among those who see themselves as organizational diagnosticians and doctors much effort is spent in trying to develop satisfying or effective relationships between members and the organization and between the organization and its environment.

This belief in the organization as a *thing* makes assessment of it relatively easy. One may ask how well the organization satisfies its members' needs, or how well it achieves its goals. Where the organization is found wanting on either count, the organization as such is revealed as needing change or improvement. Though the organizational doctors do not always agree on what to do with the diseased or ailing organization, there is no lack of prescriptions to deal with its maladies. In education, these remedies vary from those that abolish the organization to those that merely transform it in some way.

An alternative view

And yet this notion of organizations as creations apart from people, as entities capable of having goals and responding to their environment, creates a paradox. No matter how obvious their reality, nor how theoretically convenient the conception of them as such, organization theorists – if not men of practical affairs – must deal with some puzzling questions flowing from the idea of organizations as 'real' things. If organizations are real but non-human, how can they have so human a thing as a goal? And how can an organization behave, respond or adapt when these are typically properties of organisms, not things? Though there may be many analogies between organizations and organisms, or between organizations and complex interacting physical systems, it is one thing to say these systems are similar and quite another to say *they are the same*. With some notable exceptions (e.g. Cyert and March, 1963; Simon, 1964), few organization theorists begin with the notion that organization goals are ideas held in the human mind rather than a property of an abstraction – the organization itself. With few exceptions (Silverman, 1970, pp. 5–6) organization theorists fail to ask how it is that individuals perceive the goals of an organization and orient their behaviour toward it. In short, few organization theorists see organizations as categories for understanding the world of social action, as categories created by individuals and dependent upon human acceptance and support. Instead, much of organization theory deals with human *response to* organization rather than with human activity in *creating* organizations.

The difference is important. The common view of organization sees it as an external structure with rules, powers and goals of its own. It is this structure with which the individual must deal. Many critics of organization therefore see organization as inherently alien to human purpose and wish to destroy it in order to free mankind of its chains. Other critics merely wish to make organization compatible with human needs and desires. If we see organizations not as imposed on man but as created by him, we begin to ask some different questions about organizations. In this view, individuals not only create the organization, they *are* the organization. Of course, different individuals bring diverse ideas, aspirations or needs to the organization. To see organization as created out of such diversity is to recognize organization as the social reality within which individuals interact; it is to see organization as 'the everyday picture of the social world' which the individual builds and regards as merely 'what everybody knows' (Silverman, 1970, p. 6).

In answer to the first question posed at the outset of this chapter we may say that organizations have goals in the same way that individuals have goals – except that, in the organization, the individual must concern himself not only with his own goals but with those of others as well. Thus the concept of organization we are dealing with here is not a single, uniform entity, but a multifaceted notion reflecting what the individual sees as his social world and what meanings and purposes the individual brings to or takes from that reality.

Bavelas (1960, p. 498) baldly states the proposition basic to this notion of organization: 'Human organizations are not biological organisms; they are social inventions.' Following this line of thinking leads to the paradox that man not only creates his social reality, he then responds to it as something other than human invention. If organizations are a kind of invented social reality, we should seek to understand them in terms of the world-taken-for-granted by individuals involved with organizations or in terms of the individual's images of himself and of the organizations of which he is a part (cf. Silverman, 1970, pp. 143, 182, 228). With this frame of reference, we should not be surprised to find that organizational structure has no uniform effect upon people but depends upon the person perceiving it and his definition of social reality. From this vantage point, too, we would probably regard it as useless to try to deal with a single organizational structure, whether our aim was to abolish this structure, to change it or to improve it. And with this view of organization, we would probably also give up attempts to judge its effectiveness in terms of a single set of goals – whether those were external goals toward which bureaucracies are supposed to strive or goals which organizations are thought to achieve through dynamic equilibrium with their environments.

Can individual goals become organizational goals?

These considerations raise the second question posed at the beginning of this chapter: Given that individuals are in some way determinants of organization, how are goals of individuals transformed into something we recognize as goals of the organization? To me the best answer to this question – though not a complete answer – is found in the decision-making tradition in organization theory (e.g. Cyert and March, 1963; Simon, 1964; Thompson, 1967), which views organization as a social reality within which individuals see rules, pressures, demands, powers and dependencies. Organization thus becomes the perceived social reality within which individuals make decisions. The heart of this view is not a single abstraction called organization, but rather varied perceptions by individuals of what they can, should or must do in dealing with others (Silverman, 1970, p. 136). When an individual shifts his frame of reference for decision making, he shifts his organization. These ideas require us to abandon notions of organizations as striving to achieve externally set targets or achieving a simple equilibrium with the environment. Rather, the view suggested is a continuous process of bargaining and coalition among individuals. Some coalitions turn out to be viable, at least in the short run, thus giving members of those coalitions the power to allocate resources or to divide the labor in ways that seem good to them. In this view, the goals of the organization are the current preoccupations and intentions of the dominant organizational coalition. This conception of organizational goals does not require us to regard them as some ultimate point toward which the entire organization moves, nor as a steady state characterizing organization–environment relationships. Instead, organizational goals may be as fleeting as the membership of the dominant coalition; as changeable as members' views of what is practical, desirable or essential. Above all, this view of organizational goals frees us from the need to see such goals as uniform and stable throughout the organization: they are as varied and no more stable or rational than the individual.

What the proponents of this decision-making tradition in organization theory do not make clear is why and how others accept a dominant coalition's definition of a situation. Though conceiving a balance between organizational inducements and member contributions may help to resolve this problem (March and Simon, 1958, pp. 84–8), the basic difficulty remains. We must explain the common but extraordinary situation in which we find members of organizations 'actually performing tasks demanding a high degree of skill and involvement that are utterly remote from their personal interests and the rest of their cognitive field' (Burns, 1967, p. 133). To understand what is going on in organizations we must explain behavior in terms meaningful to the actors involved. Instead of prescribing what kinds of behavior *would make* a healthy organization if only people engaged in them, it might be better to find out first the motivations that do in fact act as springs for individual action.

This line of thinking takes us back to an important but often neglected idea in the work of Max Weber. Weber cast his analysis of history and organization in terms of *Verstehen*, a concept requiring that the actions of men be understood in terms meaningful to them, not in terms of values and meanings held, however dearly, by outside observers. Thus Weber (1947,

p. 113) classified organizations according to the 'validity' and 'legitimate order' that people accord them. Elaborating on this notion, Simon (1957a, p. 126; 1957b, pp. 108–110) argues that authority rests not with 'persons of authority' but in relationships built upon people's beliefs about how they should behave toward one another. In coming to believe what one *ought* to do, one also shapes a role for oneself and ultimately creates an organization in which that role may be performed. Therefore, the kinds of organization we live in derive not from their structure but from attitudes and experiences we bring to organizations from the wider society in which we live. Organizational change, then, requires more than structural change; it requires changes in the meanings and purposes that individuals learn within their society.

This notion of organizations as dependent upon meanings and purposes which individuals bring to organizations from the wider society does not require that all individuals share the same meanings and purposes. On the contrary, the views I am outlining here should make us seek to discover the varying meanings and objectives that individuals bring to the organizations of which they are a part. We should look more carefully, too, for differences in objectives between different kinds of people in organizations and begin to relate these to differences in power or access to resources.

[. . .]

Where do these ideas leave the concept of 'organization'? I began this chapter by questioning the common notion of organization as a structure with functions and goals apart from those of the individuals who inhabit it. But what is an organization if it is not something separate from individuals? At the present time, I find myself unable to answer this question satisfactorily. Burns (1967, p. 132) provides us with a beginning point when he speaks of organization as a 'transducer' connecting a set of demands with a set of action consequences. Now 'transducer' is a term from physics designating a device which receives power in one form and transforms it into another (e.g. a telephone transforms electric power into acoustic power). In organizations, the transforming mechanism lies within individuals. It is found in individuals striving to change their demands or beliefs into definitions of reality that others must regard as valid and accept as limitations on their actions. Although this concept of organization permits us to speak of the dominating demands and beliefs of some individuals, and allows us to explore how those with dominating views use the advantage of their position, we need not think of these dominating views as 'necessary', 'efficient', 'satisfying', or even 'functional', but merely as an invented social reality, which holds for a time and is then vulnerable to redefinition through changing demands and beliefs among people. Our conceptions of organizations must be as complex as the reality we try to understand.

Designing and changing organizations: Some speculations and implications

In short I have argued that we lack an adequate concept of organization, though when it comes to designing or changing organizations, we often behave as though we have one. Although organizations do not possess structures independent of people, or goals apart from human intentions, change agents strive to reshape their structures, reformulate their goals, or achieve a better integration of the individual with the structure. In opposition to these views, I have put forward an alternate but less commonly held view: that organizations are ideas held in the human mind, sets of beliefs – not always compatible – that people hold about the ways they should relate to one another. Within these relationships, people act to realize values, to attain goals important to them. This alternate view holds that there is no overriding purpose which an organization serves and no single structure through which it operates. Rather, organizations incorporate a multiplicity of ends, and uncertain means for achieving them. What are the implications of this view for organizational analysis and change strategies based upon such an analysis? The discussion will focus primarily on schools as a particular type of organization.

Received notions of organization theory

What seems extraordinary in much contemporary organizational analysis is that theories which see organizations as 'things' always seem to prevail over theories which see organizations as extensions of individuals. Traditions dealing with organizations as mechanisms or organisms usually find favor over those which, reflecting Weberian views, see organizations as complex patterns of choice made by individuals in pursuit of ends that are meaningful to them.

Facing such complexity, we should desist in our efforts to discover the 'most effective' organizational structure or the one 'best adapted to the environment' and put more effort into understanding the specific meanings, purposes and problems of specific individuals in specific organizations. Though it may move against efforts to develop a 'science' of organizations, wherein all propositions have universal force and validity, this seemingly anti-organizational view of organizations asks simply for a human perspective in understanding and assessing organizations.

Thompson (1967, pp. 84–7) has suggested that the assessment of organizations depends upon our beliefs about what an organization should do and upon our knowledge of means to achieve those ends. Where there is dispute about ends, means and outcomes – as appears to be the case with schools – we should have little faith in organizational doctors who are ready to diagnose organizational ailments and offer prescriptions for prompt recovery. Surely, as a minimum, we should be more careful than we usually are about making prescriptions for organizational change that assume similar dynamics in the operation of most, if not all, organizations. Prescriptive organization theory (e.g. Blake and Mouton, 1968; Likert, 1961) is often based almost exclusively upon the study of economic organizations; one seldom gets the feeling that prescriptions for educational change are based upon theories and conceptions of *schools*. Organizational theorists (e.g. Pugh *et al.*, 1969) seem all too ready to assume that concepts like *bureaucracy*, *participation, supervision, technology, workflow*, and a host of others have the same meaning in organizations of all kinds, regardless of the individuals involved, the goals they pursue, and the cultural environment from which they come.

[. . .]

Organizations as they are

If organization theorists and change agents took seriously the views propounded here, they would put more emphasis upon open-ended inquiry into organizations and less upon strategies for improving them. My suggestion is that present organization theory tells us too little about organizations as they really are and too much about the biases of the theorists and change agents. Thus organization theorists have spent much time saying that organizations ought to be 'healthy' or that individuals ought to find fulfillment within them. There is virtually no end to statements that organizations ought to be adapted to their environments, nor to prescriptions for improving that adaptation.

Instead of trying to build or verify more grand theory about organizations and instead of trying to remodel organizations, it might be better to find out how organizations are able to survive in their supposedly crippled, ill-adapted or non-satisfying forms. Such an investigation will take us into a study of human purpose and interaction within organization; it will take us into the study of individual reaction to role structure rather than into explanations of why certain role structures are 'necessary'. In looking at organizations more squarely as they are, we will have to start looking at schools as schools and not as some presumed sub-species of an ideal type called organization (Bidwell, 1965; Miles, 1967; Sieber, 1968). For all their acknowledged importance, it is extraordinary how little we know about schools as organizations in their own right. Instead, when we theorize about schools as organizations, we are likely to borrow ideas and models from other areas of organizational study. When we come to analyze or improve them, we are apt to reach for concepts developed to describe other kinds of organizations. Thus much of our effort to understand schools as organizations is cast in terms of bureaucratic theory, theory of general social structure, or industrial psychology and sociology. [. . .]

Understanding schools in their own terms will require more direct and active attention to understanding school experience for its own sake. For this purpose, a comparative and historical perspective is essential (cf. Mayntz, 1964; Burns, 1967). We must begin to understand more thoroughly and deeply the varieties of experience people have within the organizations we call schools, and we must not limit the experiences studied to those of particular groups. The varied and often conflicting views of teachers and administrators are important, but we also need to know about pupils, parents and school board members – and to know them within a perspective which relates these various groups to one another. We need to compare the meanings, experiences and understandings found in particular schools in one time and place with those found in other times and places. It is only through such comparison that we may come to understand the frame of reference, the world-taken-for-granted, that defines 'school'. In abandoning received theories about organizations in general and about schools in particular, we will have to look to a new kind of research – one that builds theory from the data rather than one that selects data to confirm theories developed apart from the data. This requirement directs us to theory built from observations in specific organizations; it directs us as well to understanding the actions, purposes and experiences of organizational members in terms that make sense to them (cf. Glaser and Strauss, 1967; Center for New Schools, 1972).

Excessive concern with structure and process

In recent years, change agents and practitioners have focused strongly on the internal structures and processes of organizations, a concern flowing from the belief that organizations have goals, from the belief that if we can just get the structure or process 'right', organizations will be more effective in achieving goals or better adapted to their environments. [. . .]

Radical critics of education take the concern for structure and processes one step further than more conventional organizational analysts. Where the conventional analyst is likely to strive to get the 'right' structure or process in an organization, the radical critic is apt to believe that there is something inherently wrong with organizational structure and that it exerts a baneful effect upon the human personality. The belief dies hard that organizational structure is 'real' and independent of human meaning and purpose.

[. . .]

Shifting the external trappings of organization, which we may call organization structure if we wish, turns out to be easier than altering the deeper meanings and purposes which people express through organization. Usually, we are aware of these meanings and purposes only when we try to change them in ourselves or others. Thus some radical critics of education have become painfully aware of differences between their own and others' values when they removed the conventional structures of organization. The result was not to abolish the problems they saw as inherent in structure, but to discover them in a new form. To explain this outcome, we are forced to see problems of organizational structure as inherent not in 'structure' itself, but in the human meanings and purposes which support that structure. Thus it appears that we cannot solve organizational problems by either abolishing or improving structure alone; we must also look at their human foundations.

Rationality in organizational design

[. . .]

In the conventional way of looking at organizations, we resolutely split ends and means; we insist on thinking of organizations as means for the attainment of specified goals. This view fosters rational analysis of organization: the goals provide criteria for assessing specific policies and practices and the organization itself. Such an approach lies at the base of programmed budgeting and management by objectives.

Unfortunately, these schemes assume a more rational world than actually exists, and so frequently fail. At least, they assume a different kind of rationality than usually prevails in the organizational world. In education, for example, we seem to think we need formal goals to define what goes on in schools. The assumption is that present activity is best understood not as an end in itself but as a means to an end, a means called into existence by some ultimate goal. [. . .]

But do ultimate goals actually energize the action of people involved with schools? [. . .] I am sure there are many people involved with schools for whom certain educational end-products are important goals. I am also fairly sure there are many others for whom process is more important than product. There are those among us who simply believe in 'open schools', in 'strict discipline', or in a host of other qualities they wish schools to have. And people are seldom willing to compromise or negotiate on these beliefs, as these beliefs do not represent means toward ends but ends in themselves. Thus for some of us participation, openness, authenticity and trust are good things; others may value knowledge, achievement, competition and 'high standards'. Achievement of some of these goals may be assessed 'objectively' by external evaluators, others only 'subjectively' by those involved. My point is only that we need to know more about the objectives of people in schools, and we need to discover how they change and whose goals hold the day when conflict and disagreement arise about what should be done, how, when, where and to whom. Answers to these questions may not only give us a better notion of what goes on within schools, they may also make us more cautious in assessing them, and less willing to prescribe single solutions for improving them.

Technology, goals and effectiveness

The notion of effectiveness in organizations implies accepted goals and reliable means for achieving them. Conceiving technology as 'reliable means for achieving goals' (Thompson, 1967, p. 14), conventional theory sees organizations as striving to increase the reliability of technology or to reduce the cost of its application. This notion of organizational effectiveness requires revision if we no longer assume a simple set of organization goals, nor rely on the notion of an abstract entity – the organization – which possesses them. The view of organizations as reflections of varied human purposes makes it difficult if not impossible to apply simple criteria for measurement of organizational effectiveness. The basic difficulty is that we cannot speak – as does so much of applied organization theory – about increasing organizational effectiveness, unless we achieve two clear but often neglected tasks. One is to map the versions of reality which people in school see around themselves. The second is to discover stresses and disjunctures that threaten these definitions of reality. Implied in these tasks is a third one: developing the commitment of people to new social goals and the means they consider effective for achieving them. It is my contention that we might better carry out this third task – the task of building an organization – if we complete the other two first, as we would then have a clearer picture of the existing organizational world and forces within it. Whether such knowledge permits us to speak of 'designing' organizations is still an open question, because we so poorly comprehend what is involved in that task. What seems clear is that we should view with scepticism any presumed rules for designing organizations and any presumed universal models for the good school until we know more about what people want from schools and how they believe they can attain it.

[. . .]

A problem in making organizations more 'effective' may be that many people do not hold goals for them in the sense of *ends* that the organization is to accomplish, but merely hold a set of beliefs about what it is *right* to do in an organization. The person who holds that a given percentage of the school budget should be devoted to research is expressing a belief about what it is right to do in the organization rather than a preference for an end the organization should accomplish. Such a person is satisfied – although perhaps temporarily – by the allocation of money to research, not by the product of research. It is my suspicion that many goals in education are of this type; they reflect our beliefs about the quality of experience we want in schools, the way resources are to be distributed, or the ways people should behave toward one another. For these kinds of goals, *technology is not necessary*: people in organizations are either able to express their beliefs in behavior or they are not able to do so.

Other goals in education represent ends to be accomplished in the future through the direction and co-ordination of activities in the present. Many of the standard goals of education are of this type: they describe skills to be acquired or knowledge to be attained. For these kinds of goals, technology is essential – it is an instrument for the accomplishment of the goals.

These two kinds of goals are often interwoven. For example, it is a widely accepted goal that children learn to read in school: indeed, even children may hold this goal. Such a goal describes an end-point to be attained and therefore calls into play the question of what technology is effective in teaching children to read. Inevitably, however, in trying to apply technology in pursuit of a reading goal, we will encounter other kinds of goals – goals that express people's beliefs about how that technology should be used (e.g. goals concerning the climate of the classroom in which the reading instruction takes place, or the content of the reading material itself). Rationality in the design of organizations seems to require that we separate decisions with respect to these two kinds of goals. We must ask what ends it is possible to accomplish with existing educational technology, and we must ask under what conditions we are to apply that technology. In making decisions about these two kinds of goals, we should not believe that people are invariably satisfied as long as end-point goals are achieved, nor that intended end-point goals are achieved as long as people are satisfied by current circumstances.

[. . .]

Conclusion

Most theories of organization grossly simplify the nature of the reality with which they deal. The drive to see the organization as a single kind of entity with a life of its own apart from the perceptions and beliefs of those involved in it blinds us to its complexity and the variety of organizations people create around themselves. It leads us to believe that we must change some abstract thing called 'organization' rather than socially maintained beliefs about how people should relate to one another and how they may attain desired goals. The more closely we look at organizations, the more likely we are to find expressions of diverse human meanings. The focus of investigation should not be 'What should be done to improve this organization?', but 'Whose meanings define what is right to do among people here involved with one another?' The difference in these questions is, of course, the difference between ought and is. But we do judge what is, and we do call Machiavelli immoral for separating ends and means. Yet when we come to judge our organizations, will we think of them as artifacts of human creation and remember what it is we judge? If we do, we may come to agree with Cassius:

> The fault, dear Brutus, lies not in our stars.
> But in ourselves. . . .

References

Argyris, C. *Integrating the individual and the organization.* New York: Wiley, 1964.
Ash, R. T. Durkheim's *Moral education* reconsidered: Towards the creation of a counterculture. *School Review*, November 1971, **80**, 111–42.
Bavelas, A. Leadership: Man and function. *Administrative Science Quarterly*, March 1960, **4**, 491–8.

Bennis, W. G. *Changing organizations*. New York: McGraw-Hill, 1966.

Bennis, W. G. Beyond bureaucracy. In W. G. Bennis and P. Slater, *The temporary society*. New York: Harper and Row, 1968, pp. 53–76.

Bidwell, C. E. The school as a formal organization. In J. G. March (ed.), *Handbook of organizations*. Chicago: Rand-McNally, 1965, pp. 972–1022.

Blake, R. R. and Mouton, J. S. *Corporate excellence through grid organization development: A systems approach*. Houston, Texas: Gulf Publishing Co., 1968.

Burns, T. The comparative study of organizations. In V. Vroom (ed.), *Methods of organizational research*. Pittsburgh: University of Pittsburgh Press, 1967, pp. 118–70.

Center for New Schools. Stengthening alternative high schools. *Harvard Educational Review*, August 1972, **42**, 313–50.

Cyert, R. M. and March, J. G. *A behavioral theory of the firm*. Englewood Cliffs, NJ: Prentice-Hall, 1963.

Etzioni, A. Two approaches to organizational analyses: A critique and a suggestion. *Administrative Science Quarterly*, September 1960, **5**, 257–78.

Glaser, B. G. and Strauss, A. L. *The discovery of grounded theory*. Chicago: Aldine, 1967.

Gouldner, A. W. Organizational analysis. In R. K. Merton (ed.), *Sociology today*. New York: Basic Books, 1959.

Katz, D. and Kahn, R. *The social psychology of organizations*. New York: Wiley, 1966.

Katz, M. *Class, bureaucracy, and schools*. New York: Praeger, 1971.

Likert, R. L. *New patterns of management*. New York: McGraw-Hill, 1961.

March, J. G. and Simon, H. A. *Organizations*. New York: Wiley, 1958.

Mayntz, R. The study of organizations. *Current Sociology*, 1964. **13**(3), 95–155.

Merton, R. K. *Social theory and social structure*. New York: Free Press, 1957.

Miles, M. B. Planned change and organizational health: Figure and ground. In *Change processes in the public schools*. Eugene, Oreg.: Center for the Advanced Study of Educational Administration, 1965, pp. 11–34.

Miles, M. B. Some properties of schools as social systems. In G. Watson (ed.), *Change in school systems*. Washington, DC: National Training Laboratories, 1967, pp. 1–29.

Mouzelis, N. P. *Organization and bureaucracy*. London: Routledge and Kegan Paul, 1967.

Parsons, T. Some ingredients of a general theory of formal organizations. In A. W. Halpin (ed.), *Administrative theory in education*. Chicago: Midwest Administration Center, 1958, pp. 40–72.

Perrow, C. The analysis of goals in complex organizations. *American Sociological Review*, December 1961, **26**, 855.

Perrow, C. *Organizational analysis: A sociological view*. Belmont, Calif.: Wadsworth, 1970.

Pugh, D. S., Hickson, D. J. and Hinings, C. R. An empirical taxonomy of structures of work organizations. *Administrative Science Quarterly*, 1969, **14**, 115–26.

Rothman, D. J. Of prisons, asylums, and other decaying institutions. *The Public Interest*, Winter 1972, **26**, 3–17.

Selznick, P. Foundations of the theory of organizations. *American Sociological Review*, 1948, **13**, 25–35.

Sieber, S. D. Organizational influences on innovative roles. In T. L. Eidell and J. M. Kitchel (eds), *Knowledge production and utilization in educational administration*.

Eugene, Oreg.: Center for the Advanced Study of Educational Administration, 1968, pp. 120–42.

Silverman, D. *The theory of organisations.* London: Heinemann, 1970, pp. 5–6.

Simon, H. A. *Administrative behavior,* 2nd ed. New York: Macmillan, 1957a.

Simon, H. A. Authority. In C. M. Arensberg *et al.* (eds), *Research in industrial human relations.* New York: Harper, 1957b, pp. 103–115.

Simon, H. A. On the concept of organizational goal. *Administrative Science Quarterly,* 1964, **9**, 1–22.

Thompson, J. D. *Organizations in action.* New York: McGraw-Hill, 1967.

Thompson, J. D. and McEwen, W. J. Organization goals and environment: Goal setting as an interaction process. *American Sociological Review,* 1958, **23**, 23–31.

Weber, M. *The theory of social and economic organizations.* (Talcott Parsons, ed.). London: William Hodge, 1947.

9

Teacher perspectives on pastoral care*

Ron Best, Peter Ribbins and Colin Jarvis with Diane Oddy

Accounts in context

[. . .]
Headteachers and senior staff have a vested interest in portraying their school as a 'caring' institution because their own public image, and therefore to some extent their *self-image*, depends in no small measure on the evaluation which the public at large make of the institution for which they are responsible. This is heightened when a school is in the position of Rivendell Comprehensive, battling constantly against what staff believed to be an unjustifiably poor reputation in the local community, attributable partly perhaps to its former status as *the* 'secondary modern' school, and partly to a catchment area whose socio-economic composition was the lowest in the area. But at the time of our study it was also forced into fierce competition with neighbouring schools for the dwindling supply of children resulting from the slump in the birthrate of the late 1960s. [. . .]

What a teacher *says* has to be interpreted in the light of the *context* in which he says it. A teacher may say one thing in the context of a parents' evening or in an official document about the school's policy, but say something quite to the contrary in another context where the interests he holds are better served by different sorts of statement. This raises a fundamental problem for anyone attempting to get at what 'pastoral care' *means* for teachers, how they perceive and evaluate pastoral structures and teacher roles, and how they construe particular situations and the interaction that takes place within them. We accept the force of the argument that to explain any social phenomenon it is necessary to establish the subjective meanings which relevant actors attach to that phenomenon, but it is difficult to see how

*This chapter is based on research conducted by the authors in 'Rivendell', a comprehensive school located in a London suburb.

one can establish *meanings* in any hard and fast way. 'Meanings' are not directly observable in the world like physical objects are, and it would be folly indeed to imagine that imputing meanings to actors or situations was something the researcher could lightly undertake.

The obvious course to follow is to ask the actors what they think is happening in any situation, and what they mean by the particular words and phrases they use to do so. By asking a teacher what he does and why he does it, it is possible to extract from him his 'account' of the situation or episode we are seeking to understand. Such 'accounts' may be seen as *giving sense to*, or *making sense of*, the particular phenomenon, by describing it in terms which make it comprehensible to the questioner. But they may also constitute a *justification* for the actor's actions on that occasion, giving them a *legitimacy* by demonstrating to the questioner that there were good reasons why he acted as he did. In other words, when asked to account for his actions, the actor does so by describing the situation in terms of its constituent parts, but *also* by indicating the *motives* behind the action and, perhaps, seeking the approval of the questioner by establishing the purity of his intention.

[. . .]

The problem is that an interview with an educational researcher is a *context* like any other, and is therefore the setting to which both teacher and researcher bring certain expectations and in which their interests may be best served by a particular sort of performance. It is for others to speculate about our motives as researchers, but we cannot avoid speculation about the motives of those we interviewed. It is arguable that everything a teacher says to a researcher is suspect because he enters the interview with an expectation of the sorts of things the researcher wants to hear. [. . .]

Whether he likes it or not, the researcher has to make some judgement about the reliability of the account which any individual teacher makes. [. . .] Although some kind of interpretation and evaluation of the reliability of actors' accounts is inescapable, there are ways in which this can be achieved which minimize the subjective factor. For one thing, a teacher can spend so long with the researcher over such a period of time that it is unlikely that he could maintain throughout a bogus stance adopted at the beginning. After a while the mask will begin to slip. We found that teachers tended to relax a little more each time they were interviewed, and as changing conditions in the school became matters of personal concern to them, so they began to talk less in the educationist jargon, and more about their own feelings and attitudes as *people*. [. . .]

In our research we spent 2 years in Rivendell Comprehensive, interviewing 59 of the 82 staff, and observing teachers in a variety of situations, including form periods, parents' evenings, staff meetings and visits to feeder schools, and in informal settings in the staffroom and elsewhere. A total of 77 reports of observations were compiled by the research team over the 2-year period, and these provide a good background against which to evaluate the accounts teachers gave in interviews. At the same time, we were able to compare the accounts of each teacher against those of others, and the different accounts the same teacher gave on different occasions. Where there were inconsistencies within or between teachers' accounts, or where their accounts did not match up with what we observed, further interviews were held to follow up the discrepancy. In this way, we were able to reach a position in which we are fairly confident of the validity of the interpretations we finally made.

The educationist context

Although all our interviews with Rivendell teachers could be said to take place in the 'educationist context', this was sometimes made fairly explicit by the questions which we asked. In particular, we asked a number of teachers two questions which might have signalled to them that an 'educationist' answer was expected:

1 Would you say that the school has a general philosophy or policy on pastoral care, and if so what is it?
2 If I asked you to give me a definition of 'pastoral care' what would you say?

It is possible to interpret responses to these questions as drawing upon the vocabulary of the 'conventional wisdom' of the literature, and concurring with the official statements of the school's policy documents. Thus expression was often given to the idea of 'caring' for the 'welfare' of the 'whole child', with every teacher a 'pastoral teacher'. But further insights can be gained from deeper analysis of these and other answers to these 'educationist' questions.

Although teachers were willing to give expression to the indivisibility of the 'pastoral' and the 'academic' in the school's provision, and of the individual pupil into the 'learner' and the 'child', some teachers did identify 'pastoral care' as something distinctive and separate. Thus, Mrs Taylor defined 'pastoral care' as a task – 'to look after the emotional and physical needs of the individual' – while Mrs Plummer defined it as 'caring for the child, knowing about its home background and really problems they have in school which aren't academic . . .' For some teachers at any rate, 'pastoral care' has to do with the welfare of the child as a *child* rather than as merely a pupil who might have academic problems. [. . .]

Teacher perspectives

We have noted that the accounts teachers give in interviews are to some extent a function of the kind of question which the researcher asks, and for this reason questions have to be very carefully phrased. We tried to ask a good many questions that were fairly open-ended to allow teachers a reasonably free rein in deciding what they wanted to talk about, though more direct and even 'pointed' questions were employed in subsequent interviews in order to follow up points of interest or discrepancies between or within accounts and between accounts and observations. This permitted teachers to range quite widely in the issues they chose to discuss, albeit in an interview they knew to be part of a research project on 'pastoral care'. In the event, teachers used this setting to talk about a considerable variety of topics including the curriculum, grouping practices, the school as an administrative structure, and problems of teacher discipline and classroom control. In analysing our field-notes and transcripts of interviews, we found a number of distinct perspectives emerging.

Children as persons

The *child-centred* perspective presented in the 'educationist' context was sustained by some teachers in response to questions about their own jobs. For example, when Mrs Phillips was asked what sorts of problems she might discuss with parents, she gave the following reply:

> For example, how long a kid may sit at home worrying about his homework before he actually picks up a pen and does it. A child may sit for three or four hours. Once I know about this I can slant his homework in such a way as to help him over it. . . .
>
> I have a girl who was a battered baby . . . she is very much a 'loner'. She has a bowel problem as well which makes her unpopular with the other children . . . every time she had a PE period she would run away. When I asked her why, all she would say was 'I hate this school'. I got some of the girls together and talked about how we needed to convince her that we liked her. The girls cooperated in this. Now she doesn't run away. . . . Now she thinks she likes the school.

In both these extracts, the problems being dealt with are the problems of the child as a *person*: they are problems of personal happiness and adaptation. What some teachers might perceive as an *academic* problem in the poor quality of homework or as a *disciplinary* problem in 'ducking' a PE lesson were, for this teacher, emotional, social and physical problems with which the child needed help. In both cases, the solution was to be found in an adaptation on the part of the teacher, by 'slanting' the homework in such a way that it ceased to threaten the child, and by encouraging her peer-group (the form) to make her feel wanted. The second example shows considerable sensitivity on the part of the teacher who perceived the problem as, among other things, an *interpersonal* one, and adopted an interpersonal strategy to help resolve it. Moreover, the importance of the child's own perception of the problem was recognized as, for example, when 'I hate school' was taken as admissible evidence in analysing and attacking the problem.

[. . .]

Several other teachers adopted this kind of perspective in answers to a wide variety of questions. Mr Byford, for example, said he 'firmly believed that kids don't misbehave in class unless there is a problem behind it', while Miss Rawlings welcomed the extra form periods of the new system as giving her time to sort out children's problems, something which was particularly important as the counsellor was leaving. Mr Forbes expected teachers in his House to 'be involved with children' during form periods in order 'to get a better understanding of the children', and saw the value of parents' evenings as bound up with parental anxiety and peace of mind, and in coming to a deeper understanding of the children themselves:

> I presume this to be a general idea across the Houses: to reassure parents that their kids are settling in and are able to settle in reasonably well. Basically it is to set their minds at rest, and if it helps us to understand the kids better as well, that's all to the good.

Children as pupils

A nice distinction can be made between such a child–centred position and what might be termed the *pupil-centred perspective* which other teachers employed. For although many teachers did seem to orientate their comments to those for whose welfare the school supposedly exists, not all of them perceived their charges as *children* or *persons*, but rather concerned themselves mainly or exclusively with the child in his academic role as the pupil. Such teachers saw the emotional and personal problems of children not as some-how exclusively 'pastoral', but as stemming from the pedagogical practices of the teachers themselves. Both the organization of the curricular content and the teachers' classroom practice were viewed in this way. For example, Mr Stephens commented that all schools to some extent teach children 'the pleasure of success and the pain of failure', but that the element of pain could be reduced by sensitive teaching methods: 'If you just go around the class and ask questions some children will experience the pleasure of knowing the answer and others will have a very different emotional experience.' The same applied to behavioural problems: 'I think you have got to be very careful and check that it is not the content of the course, the way it is taught or how it is organized that contributes to the child's behaviour which has led to it being labelled.' For other teachers, like Mrs Hobbs, the pastoral provision had ultimately to be seen in its function as a facilitator of a pupil's academic performance: 'What you have to do is to try to get to a position where the child can do his best work. . . . To get the best work you must care for the child.' Although both these teachers are expressing a concern for pupil welfare, their comments 'home in' on the experiences of the pupil as a *learner* and how the teacher can best bring learning about.

One senior teacher (Mr Bailey) with many years of experience as a head of house, head of year, and teacher of numerous subjects, epitomized this perspective. Speaking of the integrated humanities course which made extensive use of 'key' lessons and workcards, he was critical of the previous director of studies who, he said, 'did not read enough education'. If he had, he would have known that:

> . . . one-hour long 'key' lessons are not really as educational as Mr Jarrett thought. Ten to twelve minutes *doing* something which is immediately followed up by the *kids* doing it would be more educational. The 'key' lesson loses its impact – even films have no impact due to children's exposure to televison – and often isn't followed up for days. . . .
> (Moreover) the workcard system can lead to wholesale copying of work from books. Added to this is the fact that a teacher who attempts to discuss the work with a kid may be an intrusion that is resented.

[. . .]

Although willing to categorize children as 'bright' or 'dim' and to criticize mixed-ability grouping, this was again accompanied by statements about the learning implications of such groupings and the appropriate course of action the teacher should take:

> The contrast between bright and dim in the same class day after day is very damaging, at least as damaging as the stigma that attaches to the G stream in a streamed school. In the mixed-ability classes the very bright and the very dim both suffer, and if I have to concentrate my attention on one or the other I go for the dimmer ones on the grounds that the bright ones have got enough about them to be able to catch up and make up for the attention they do not get.

In these extracts we see repeated references to the activities of teaching and learning *from the position of the learner*. Particular teaching methods like 'key' lessons and workcards are evaluated in terms of the motivation and span of attention of the learner, and in their unintended consequences in, for example, 'wholesale copying'. The strengths and weaknesses of mixed-ability grouping and child-centred methods are discussed in terms of their implications for successful learning. [. . .] There is an emphasis throughout on the structuring of knowledge in the light of children's age and ability, and of effects of good structuring and sensitive practice on the pupil's acquisition of essential skills and growing confidence, while an overall philosophy which caters for the development of both creativity and 'the basics' is advocated. Though in some respects a formal-traditional teacher, his attitudes are based in a thoughtful consideration of the pupil's requirements. Not surprisingly he saw the appropriateness of pastoral systems as determined by the development of the child, preferring the year system to the house system.

> because you work in age-groups and this is the more natural way to group them pastorally. You work in different ways with kids of

different ages. The psychological development of children is important in how you deal with them and this goes with age.

Such a perspective we may term *pupil-centred*.

Teachers as disciplinarians

The *child-centred* and *pupil-centred* perspectives stand in stark contrast to the *discipline-centred perspective* of a number of other teachers. In the context of interviews which they knew to be about 'pastoral care', some teachers chose to talk a good deal of the time about problems of the teacher's control in the classroom and the problems posed for it by the failure of other staff to give them the necessary backing. Although such teachers did go on to talk about the problems with which children might need help, it is significant that the 'problems' which they chose first to talk about, or talked most about, were their own problems of 'sorting out' naughty children and getting 'backing' for their sanctions. For example, when asked about her role as a second-year form tutor Mrs Plummer replied:

> I don't teach my form so I don't get to know them so well. It involves trying to help them with anything in or out of school, anything they want to ask me about. Some are more forthcoming than others. For example, a boy came up to me the other day and said 'My Mum went off last night.' There are some family problems like this. . . .

So far so good, but

> Mrs Plummer: . . . then there are school problems, for example, if they are in trouble with another teacher. If it comes to my attention I say 'I don't want children in my class to be in trouble'. If they get into trouble I tell them I will do something about it; that is, not only will the teacher punish them but I will punish them as well. For example, I may see a child put out of the class.
>
> Interviewer: As regards the boy whose Mum's gone off, what do you do and what do you think the kid expects you to do when he tells you about it?
>
> Mrs Plummer: This varies from child to child. I know one child who expected his form tutor to take the place of his mother, but I wouldn't want to get that close, it's dangerous. If you get too close your working relationship breaks down. It's OK in the first year but by the fourth year there would be problems. Children would take advantage of you after a while. *I think you would have discipline problems.* [our italics]

In this extract, the teacher begins with an apparently child-centred response but quickly moves on to talk about 'school problems' which turn out to be problems of pupil discipline and teacher control. Thus, when a child from her form is 'in trouble with another teacher', she does not talk to the child to try to pinpoint the source of the problem from the child's point of view, as might Mrs Phillips for example, but 'backs up' the other teacher's authority by threatening further punishment. The interviewer's attempt to develop the question of 'home problems' only led to her arguing a case for social distance between the form tutor and her class, on the grounds that the alternative would only lead to *discipline* problems. Not surprisingly, Mrs Plummer went on to describe the role of the head of year as essentially disciplinary and as the 'immediate solution' for problems of misbehaviour. If the head of year proved ineffective, she said she 'might also *use* Mr Piper, my Head of Department'. This concept of using other staff is one which other teachers employed and, as we shall see, is indicative of an attitude towards middle-management as primarily 'there' to be 'used' by the teacher to resolve his or her problems of control.

This applied also to Mr Carroll, a sixth-form tutor, who described the house and year systems in terms of their effectiveness as a disciplinary back-up: [. . .]

Interviewer: What is it that distinguishes the vertical from the horizontal structure? Is there something distinct in their function?

Mr Carroll: Very little. It's a very good question. As far as I can see, there is little in the way of distinguishing features between them. In individual cases *the Head of House may be stronger than the Head of Year, so you go to the former. At least this arrangement gives you two bites at the cherry: if one doesn't pay off the other does.* [our italics]

[. . .]

For Mr Carroll the dual system of houses and years was seen as giving him 'two bites at the cherry' when seeking backing for disciplinary matters, or, as he said later, it 'gives you two levers on the child'. [. . .]

This concern with discipline was also expressed by some teachers in positions of considerable authority. In particular, Mrs Marshall [. . .] (whose position was sometimes described as 'Assistant Head of Upper School with special responsibility for senior girls' welfare') said her job was 'to keep an eye on how successfully the children settle down into the adult role' and that to do this she had to 'put the screws on' when necessary:

When a teacher needs an ultimate deterrent they send the child to me. If it is a serious problem, e.g. girls truanting yesterday, I make contact immediately with the parents. In such cases I contact the House Head to put together information on the case. Children know if Mrs Marshall catches you you automatically have a detention to make up the time lost. The biggest part of the punishment is that I record it. I have a thirty-year reputation as a disciplinarian, known to be firm and fair. The children know it is a 'fair cop'.

Like a number of other teachers, Mrs Marshall did make comments with a less disciplinary flavour, for example:

> In the Upper School both the Year Heads could not help but be concerned about welfare, they are that sort of person. The caring teacher could not help but be drawn into it.

But she could also describe her *modus operandi* in the following terms:

> When classes are sensible and responsible I am friendly and we have a happy time; when classes are childish and stupid I am a bitch. There was one class, the only case in all my time at the school, where I had to be unpleasant for two years.

On balance, her attitude to discipline is one of seeking compliance on the part of the children, and she takes her responsibility for 'senior girls' welfare' to be primarily a disciplinary one, characterized by 'firmness' and 'fairness', but entailing automatic punishments for certain offences and being 'a bitch' when classes buck her authority. [. . .]

For Mr Rutledge, the pre-eminent concern was how to make his sanctions 'stick', in particular how to get the backing of senior staff in ensuring that children turn up for detention. This was very evident when he was asked for his views on the new 'social and pastoral organization' of the school:

> I don't really give those things a lot of thought, *provided I know who's in what position so that if I have trouble I know who to go to*. There is an obvious advantage in having a clear structure which I know is there and the kids know is there. *It is important in following up sanctions*. I take it it's the hierarchy you are talking about. If a child doesn't turn up for detention I go to the Head of Department. . . . Say I've put a boy on detention, and he doesn't turn up, I refer him to the Head of Department. I like to have the child myself in detention, so (the Head of Department) may say he is going to come to your detention at such and such a time. . . .
>
> I have also had dealings recently with Mrs Sanders as Assistant Head of Middle School. It is a similar thing; if I had a problem with a particular boy, say I put him on detention and he didn't turn up. I would refer the boy to her. [our italics]
>
> [. . .]

And later, commenting on the relative simplicity of the new structure, he said:

> Well if you have a Head of Year and an Assistant, a Head of House and an Assistant, a Head of Department and a Head of Subject, etc. *and you try to carry out your sanctions*, I did find occasions that there might be

some problem over who the problem ought to be referred to, and some people might be *over-used*. For example, Mr Kitson, as Head of Lower School, was over-used, and he told me on one occasion to refer a particular problem to the Head of House and not to him. I try to deal with it myself as my problem, and only if it gets out of hand, *if they don't turn up*, then I refer it. *Detention is the heaviest sanction I can carry out.* [our italics]

Here we see Mr Rutledge returning again to the prime cause of his concern – back-up for attendance at detentions – and we also see another reference to 'using' senior teachers in this way, and all in the context of questions about what purports to be a pastoral-care system. We shall see later that Mr Rutledge was not alone in perceiving the new system in this way, and that it is arguable that it was, primarily, a structure designed to administer and facilitate better discipline, but it was presented officially as a *pastoral* system. Mr Rutledge was not so much perceptive of the 'latent functions' of such systems as simply expressing what was, for him, an abiding concern with his own authority. This is typical of what we may call a *discipline-centred perspective*.

Teachers as administrators

A fourth perspective which seems to be adopted by some staff is that of the teacher concerned primarily with the efficiency and efficacy of the school as an administrative organization. [. . .] One senior member of staff (Mr Farley) who had recently attended a course in educational management and was subsequently to find himself in an important administrative position, was particularly concerned with such questions: [. . .]

The whole thing seems incredibly complex to me . . . it's incredibly complicated. Some people seem to think that the more complicated a system is, the better it is. Whether you do it vertically or horizontally, it needs to be *clear cut*. For example, eight or ten people as pastoral heads and deputies, whether as Year Heads or House Heads wouldn't matter much. . . . [our italics]

While this was not the case, a clear structure of roles and role-requirements could not exist. Instead, there would be a duplication of duties and job-specifications that only created confusion:

The dual responsibility structure of horizontal and vertical systems made the roles (of Head of House and Head of Year) unclear as well. For example, on registration, Heads of House used to send a member of their House who was not a form tutor along to register a class if the form tutor was away. Then Heads of Year were created and you got the position where both Heads of House and Heads of Year would send someone along to register the same class.

[. . .]

These sentiments were echoed by the new Head:

> The problems here were the existence of a House system and a Year system and a school system, as well as teachers with other specialist responsibilities. My difficulty as a new Head was to try to understand the system. . . . It was too complicated, there was no documentation, no flowcharts. . . . One of the great weaknesses of the existing system is its extremely inadequate documentation. . . .

But it was not only senior management who dwelt upon these sorts of problem. A junior member of staff (Mr Scott) observed:

> At the moment there are too many people; for example, a fifth-form tutor may have to contact Farley as Head of Humanities, Bailey as Head of Year, and Austen as Head of House, on a problem that a child has in Humanities. . . . This is an instance of increasing bureaucracy in schools.

And another commented:

> The school's idea of a cross-structure of Houses and Years is that there is a net to catch people, but in fact things tend to get overlooked. Each person thinks someone else is taking care of it. . . . The problem is communication, letting other people know you are doing it.

That so many staff were willing to talk about the efficiency of the administration is not surprising. [. . .] But it is also true that some teachers, of whom Mr Farley is an example, spoke almost exclusively in these sorts of terms. The references to 'tidying up' the system and to problems of 'communication' and job-specification, the importance given by teachers to clarity of roles and responsibilities, and to the need for 'documentation', and the references to 'unwieldy bureaucracies' and duplication of responsibilities, all point to a concern for a system of rational and effective administrative units. [. . .] What is particularly significant for our present discussion is the fact that the evaluations these teachers made of the *pastoral* structures were not made in terms of their effectiveness as welfare systems, but purely in terms of their administrative efficiency. Because such an attitude reflects the preoccupations of administrators, we shall refer to this as an *administrator-centred perspective*.

Teachers as academics

One teacher (Mrs Penfold) stood out from the rest because of her tendency to emphasize her role as the teacher of a *subject* rather than as a teacher of pupils or a 'carer' for children. The pastoral arrangements of the school did not seem to hold any importance for her, and she was simply uninterested in her own pastoral role as a form tutor. After 4 weeks of the autumn term she was still uncertain of the name of her form, and made little effort to use form periods for pastoral purposes or for the democratic discussion for which they were intended:

> I have a third year group – 3w1 I think – they are not all that easy. I read them ghost stories. Some teachers can do discussions; I can't; they show contempt for each other's comments. In a class of thirty it's difficult to hold discussions. One or two monopolize. . . .

She disparaged the kind of warm relationship with individual pupils which others saw as a prerequisite for helping with problems:

> I know the fifth- and sixth-year pupils very well. I have taught them for years. Some of them would discuss their problems with me. I feel strongly about intruding into pupils' lives; if they come to me it's OK. Sometimes teachers pretend a jolly old friendship with pupils of 17 or 18 that they don't really mean. It is still a pupil–teacher situation.

[. . .]

When talking to children with 'problems', these were typically described in the context of her work as a subject teacher:

> Interviewer: Do these children ever come to you with problems?
> Mrs Penfold: When I had the same class for Humanities they did, and in the class I teach some do. I had one boy in the class who was awful, very disruptive. It came out in staff-room chat that he was of very low ability. I could have looked him up in the records but it didn't dawn on me.

[. . .]

Her accounts also betray a concern with her self-image and public image as a subject specialist. She made several references to *her* option, and was anxious to defend her subject in terms of examination results:

> Mr Caldwell makes statements on the school's exam results; he says they are not good. This is rubbish, at least in Humanities.

and her guidance role in the careers 'team' and in the options programme was limited to her expertise as a subject specialist with a record of success:

> I will advise on university courses I know best from past pupils; this will be informal advice. I talk to all the third years about English Lit. options. If you teach them Humanities you are in the best position to advise them.

In some respects her position has something in common with the pupil-centred perspective of Mr Bailey. Both were concerned to talk about the academic side of the teacher's work, and made reference to the academic ability of children. But there seems to be a crucial difference, for whereas Mr Bailey talked about the *processes* by which children learn, and the implications of these for the pedagogic practice of the teacher, these matters were notably absent from Mrs Penfold's accounts. [. . .] For Mr Bailey, the focus of attention is the *pupil*; for Mrs Penfold it is the *subject*. A useful distinction can therefore be made between the pupil-centred perspective and the *subject-centred perspective*.

Multiple realities

The emphasis which our approach has given to the meanings which teachers give to their daily experience, and the opportunities given them in deciding which aspects of that experience they wish to discuss in the interview situation, led to some very wide-ranging discussions of what goes on in Rivendell Comprehensive. Not surprisingly, different teachers chose to concentrate on different facets of the school and of their work within it, from the roles of pastoral staff, through curriculum content, to methods of instruction.

It is possible to imagine hypothetical teachers – 'ideal types' in the jargon – whose perception of their situation is always in terms of one particular aspect of the school and one particular aspect of the role they play within it. For example, a teacher who perceived his work as always a question of bringing about the learning of a particular subject through appropriate and careful structuring of pedagogy and content, would be an ideal type 'pupil-centred teacher'. Whether there are actual teachers who correspond exactly to these 'ideal types' is unlikely – the teacher's role is too complex for such a unidimensional attitude to be possible on every issue – but teachers certainly vary in terms of which features of their situation they choose to stress, and the degree to which their attention is focused on only one feature. Certainly, Mr Rutledge comes very close to the ideal type 'discipline-centred teacher', and Mr Farley to the 'administrator-centred', but whether they would still appear so if interviewed or observed in other contexts is difficult to say.

What is clear, however, is that teacher perspectives in terms of the kind of emphasis they give to different aspects of the school and of the teacher's role are many and varied. [. . .] Each teacher has a *unique* perspective on the school and his place within it; there are, if you like, as many 'realities' as there are teachers, and it is arguable that any kind of categorization of perspective does violence to the subtlety and uniqueness of each teacher's understanding of his world.

Some generalizations are necessary, however, if research data is not to be left as a 'buzzing confusion' of specifics. It needs to be put into a form which will be useful for understanding the deeper structures which underlie teachers' accounts. The identification of different teacher perspectives in the language and emphasis of teachers' comments is a helpful first step towards such generalizations. In identifying *child-centred, pupil-centred, discipline-centred, administrator-centred* and *subject-centred perspectives*, we have narrowed down somewhat the field of 'multiple realities' and set the scene for locating teacher attitudes to pastoral care in the wider context of teacher roles and ideologies.

10

Leadership and ambiguity

Michael D. Cohen and James G. March

Some introductory conclusions

[. . .]

The American college and university belong to a class of organizations that can be called *organized anarchies*. By an organized anarchy we mean any organizational setting that exhibits the following general properties:

1 *Problematic goals.* It is difficult to impute a set of goals to the organization that satisfies the standard consistency requirements of theories of choice. The organization appears to operate on a variety of inconsistent and ill-defined preferences. It can be described better as a loose collection of changing ideas than as a coherent structure. It discovers preferences through action more often than it acts on the basis of preferences.
2 *Unclear technology.* Although the organization manages to survive and (where relevant) produce, it does not understand its own processes. Instead, it operates on the basis of a simple set of trial-and-error procedures, the residue of learning from the accidents of past experiences, imitation and the inventions born of necessity.
3 *Fluid participation.* The participants in the organization vary among themselves in the amount of time and effort they devote to the organization; individual participants vary from one time to another. As a result, standard theories of power and choice seem to be inadequate; and the boundaries of the organization appear to be uncertain and changing.

These properties are not limited to educational institutions; but they are particularly conspicuous there. The American college or university is a prototypic organized anarchy. It does not know what it is doing. Its goals are either vague or in dispute. Its technology is familiar but not understood. Its major participants wander in and out of the organization. These factors do not make a university a bad organization or a disorganized one; but they do make it a problem to describe, understand and lead. As a result, it is impossible for us to consider the American college presidency without making some rudimentary attempts to develop a theory of organized anarchy.

With respect to a behavioral theory of organizations, we need to investigate two major phenomena that are critical to an understanding of the kind of organizations described above. First, we need a better understanding of the processes used to make choices without the guidance of consistent, shared goals. It is clear that organizations sometimes make choices without clear goals. Decision making under ambiguity is common in complex organizations, particularly those outside the sector of private enterprise. Decisions appear often to be made without recourse either to explicit markets or to explicit bargaining (the two processes most commonly cited as procedures for decision making in the absence of consensus). Secondly, we need to study the process by which members of the organization are activated, by which occasional members become active ones, by which attention is directed toward, or away from, the organization. Not everyone in an organization is attending to everything all the time; and we need to understand how to predict the attention pattern within the organization.

With respect to normative theory, organized anarchies pose three major problems. First, we need to develop a normative theory of intelligent decision making in situations in which goals are unknown (i.e. under ambiguity). Can we provide some meaning for *intelligence* that does not depend on relating current action to known goals? We are convinced it is possible. We are far from certain what the theory will look like. Secondly, we need a normative theory of attention. Managers and others who might participate in an organization operate within the constraint of a scarce resource – the attention they can devote to the various things demanding their attention. In organizations such as those described above, in which a substantial part of the variability in behavior stems from variations in who is attending to what, decisions about the allocation of attention are primary. Thirdly, organized anarchies require a new theory of management. Much of our present theory of management introduces mechanisms for control and co-ordination that assume the existence of well-defined goals and technology, as well as substantial participant involvement in the affairs of the organization. When goals and technology are hazy and participation is fluid, many of the axioms and standard procedures of management collapse.

[. . .]

The basic ideas

When we look at universities as they struggle with the problems of reorganization, reform, choice and survival, we are struck by one quite consistent theme – decision opportunities are fundamentally ambiguous stimuli (Cohen *et al.*, 1972).* Although organizations can often be viewed as vehicles for solving well-defined problems and as structures within which conflict is resolved through bargaining, they are also sets of procedures through which organizational participants arrive at an interpretation of what they are doing and what they have done while doing it. From this point of view, an organization is a collection of choices looking for problems, issues and feelings looking for decision situations in which they might be aired, solutions looking for issues to which they might be the answer, and decision makers looking for work.

Such a view of organizational choice focuses attention on the ways in which the meaning of choice changes over time. It calls attention to the strategic effects of timing (in the introduction of choices and problems), the time pattern of available energy, and the impact of organizational structure on these.

A key to understanding the processes within organizations is to view a choice opportunity (an occasion on which an organization is expected to produce a decision) as a garbage can into which various problems and solutions are dumped by participants. The mix of garbage in a single can depends partly on the labels attached to the alternative cans; but it also depends on what garbage is being produced at the moment, on the mix of cans available, and on the speed with which garbage is collected and removed from the scene.

Although we may imagine that choice opportunities lead first to the generation of decision alternatives, then to an examination of the consequences of those alternatives, then to an examination of the consequences in terms of objectives, and finally to a decision, such a model is often a poor description of what actually happens. In a garbage can situation, a decision is an outcome (or an interpretation) of several relatively independent 'streams' within an organization.

We will limit our attention to the interrelations among four such streams:

1 *Problems*. Problems are the concern of people inside and outside the organization. They arise over issues of lifestyle; family; frustrations of work; careers; group relations within the organization; distribution of status, jobs, and money; ideology; or current crises of mankind as interpreted by the mass media or the nextdoor neighbor. All require attention. Problems are, however, distinct from choices; and they may not be resolved when choices are made.
2 *Solutions*. A solution is somebody's product. A computer is not just a solution to a problem in payroll management, discovered when needed. It is an answer actively looking for a question. The creation of need is not a curiosity of the market in consumer products; it is a general phenomenon of processes of choice. Despite the dictum that you cannot find the answer

* This chapter draws heavily on work we have done jointly with Johan Olsen.

until you have formulated the question well, you often do not know what the question is in organizational problem solving until you know the answer.

3 *Participants.* Participants come and go. Because every entrance is an exit somewhere else, the distribution of entrances depends on the attributes of the choice being left as much as it does on the attributes of the new choice. Substantial variation in participation stems from other demands on the participants' time (rather than from features of the decision under study).

4 *Choice opportunities.* These are occasions when an organization is expected to produce behavior that can be called a decision. Opportunities arise regularly, and any organization has ways of declaring an occasion for choice. Contracts must be signed; people hired, promoted, or fired; money spent; and responsibilities allocated.

Although not completely independent of each other, each of the streams can be viewed as independent and exogenous to the system. Attention will be concentrated here on examining the consequences of different rates and patterns of flows in each of the streams and different procedures for relating them.

The properties of universities as organized anarchies make the garbage can ideas particularly appropriate to an understanding of organizational choice within higher education. Although a college or university operates within the metaphor of a political system or a hierarchical bureaucracy, the actual operation of either is considerably attenuated by the ambiguity of college goals, by the lack of clarity in educational technology, and by the transient character of many participants. In so far as a college is correctly described as an organized anarchy, a college president needs to understand the consequences of a garbage can decision process.

Implications of the ideas

Elsewhere (Cohen *et al.*, 1972) we have detailed the development of these basic ideas into a computer simulation model that has been run under conditions simulating a variety of different organizational structures. This garbage can model of choice operates under each of the hypothesized organization structures to assign problems and decision makers to choices, to determine the energy required and effective energy applied to choices, to make such choices and resolve such problems as the assignments and energies indicate are feasible.

For each run of the model we have computed five simple summary statistics to describe the process:

1 *Decision style.* Within a garbage can process, decisions are made in three different ways:

(a) By *oversight*. If a choice is activated when problems are attached to other choices and if there is energy available to make the new choice quickly, it will be made without any attention to existing problems and with a minimum of time and energy.

(b) By *flight*. In some cases, choices are associated with problems (unsuccessfully) for some time until a choice 'more attractive' to the problems comes along. The problems leave the choice, and thereby make it possible to make the decision. The decision resolves no problems (they having now attached themselves to a new choice).

(c) By *resolution*. Some choices resolve problems after some period of working on them. The length of time may vary greatly (depending on the number of problems). This is the familiar case that is implicit in most discussion of choice within organizations.

Some choices involve both flight and resolution (i.e. some problems leave, the remainder are solved). We have defined these as resolution, thus slightly exaggerating the importance of that style. As a result of that convention, the three styles are mutually exclusive and exhaustive with respect to any one choice; but the same organization may use any one of them on different choices. Thus, we can describe the decision-making style of the organization by specifying the proportion of completed choices that are made in each of these three ways.

2 *Problem activity*. We wish to find some measure of the degree to which problems are active within the organization. Such a measure should reflect something like the degree of conflict within the organization or the degree of articulation of problems. We have taken the number of time periods that each problem is active and attached to some choice, and added them together to obtain the total time periods for all problems.

3 *Problem latency*. A problem may be active but not attached to any choice. It may be recognized and accepted by some part of the organization but may not be considered germane to any available choice. Presumably, an organization with relatively high problem latency will exhibit somewhat different symptoms from one with low latency. We have measured problem latency by taking the total number of periods that each problem is active but not attached to a choice and added them together to obtain the total time periods for all problems.

4 *Decision-maker activity*. To measure the degree of decision-maker activity in the system, we require some measure that reflects decision-maker energy expenditure, movement and persistence. We have computed the total number of times that any decision maker shifts from one choice to another.

5 *Decision difficulty*. We want to be able to characterize the ease with which a system makes decisions. Because of the way in which decisions can be made in the system (see the above discussion of decision style), that is not the same as the level of problem activity. We have used, as a measure, the total number of periods that each choice is active, and we added them together to obtain the total number of periods for all choices.

These summary statistics, along with a more intensive look at the individual histories of the simulations, reveal eight major properties of garbage can decision processes (for a discussion of alternative measures, see Cohen *et al.*, 1972):

1 Resolution of problems is not the most common style for making decisions except under conditions where flight is severely restricted or under a few conditions of light load. In each of our cases there were 20 problems and 10 choices. Although the mean number of choices not made was only 1.0, the mean number of problems not solved was 12.3. Decision making by flight and oversight is a major feature of the process in general. The behavioral and normative implications of a decision process that appears to make choices in large part by the flight of problems or by oversight may be particularly important for university presidents to consider.

2 The process is thoroughly and generally sensitive to variations in load. An increase in the net energy load on the system generally increases problem activity, decision-maker activity, decision difficulty, and the uses of flight and oversight. Problems are less likely to be solved, decision makers are likely to shift from one problem to another more frequently, choices are likely to take longer to make and to be less likely to resolve problems.

3 Decision makers and problems tend to *track* each other through choices. Both decision makers and problems tend to move together from choice to choice. As a result, decision makers may be expected to feel that they are always working on the same problems in somewhat different contexts, mostly without results. Problems, in a similar fashion, meet the same people wherever they go with the same result.

4 There are some important interconnections among three key aspects of the 'efficiency' of the decision processes we have specified. The first of these is problem activity – the amount of time unresolved problems are actively attached to choice situations. Problem activity is a rough measure of potential for decision conflict in the organization. It assesses the degree of involvement of problems in choices. The second aspect is problem latency – the amount of time that problems spend activated but not linked to choices. The third aspect is decision time – the persistence of choices. Presumably, a good organizational structure would keep both problem activity and problem latency low through rapid problem solution in its choices. In the garbage can process we never observe this. Some structures reduce the number of unresolved problems active in the organization but at the cost of increasing the latency period of problems and (in most cases) the time devoted to reaching decisions. Other structures decrease problem latency, but at the cost of increasing problem activity and decision time.

5 The decision-making process is frequently sharply interactive. Although some phenomena associated with the garbage can are regular and flow through nearly all the cases (for example, the effect of overall load), other phenomena are much more dependent on the particular combination of

structures involved. In fact, the process is one that often looks capricious to an observer. Many of the outcomes are produced by distinct consequences of the particular time phasing of choices, problems and participant availability.

6 Important problems are more likely to be solved than unimportant ones. Early-arriving problems are more likely to be resolved than later ones. The system, in effect, produces a queue of problems in terms of their importance – to the strong disadvantage of late-arriving, relatively unimportant problems, particularly when load is heavy. This queue is the result of the operation of the model. It was not imposed as a direct assumption.

7 Important choices are much *less* likely to resolve problems than are unimportant choices. Important choices are made by oversight and flight. Unimportant choices are made by resolution. The differences are substantial. Moreover, they are not connected to the entry times of the choices. We believe this property of important choices in a garbage can decision process can be naturally and directly related to the phenomenon in complex organizations of 'important' choices that often appear to just 'happen'.

8 Although a large proportion of the choices are made, the choice failures that do occur are concentrated among the most important and least important choices. Choices of intermediate importance are virtually always made.

In a broad sense, these features of the decision-making process provide some clues to how organizations survive when they do not know what they are doing. Much of the process violates standard notions of how decisions ought to be made. But most of those notions are built on assumptions that cannot be met under the conditions we have specified. When objectives and technologies are unclear, organizations are charged to discover some alternative decision procedures that permit them to proceed without doing violence to the domains of participants or to their model of an organization. It is a difficult charge, to which the process we have described is a partial response.

At the same time, the details of the outcomes clearly depend on features of the organizational structure. The same garbage can process results in different behavioral symptoms under different levels of load on the system or different designs of the structure of the organization. These differences raise the possibility of predicting variations in decision behavior in different organizations. [. . .]

Although there is great variability among colleges and universities, we think the model's major attributes have fairly general relevance to decision making in higher education. University decision making frequently does not 'resolve' problems. Choices are likely to be made by flight or oversight. University decision processes appear to be sensitive to changes in load. Active decision makers and problems seem often to track one another through a series of choices without appreciable progress in solving problems. Important choices seem particularly likely not to solve problems.

What we see, both in the model and in actual observations of universities, are decisions whose interpretations continually change during the process of resolution. Problems, choices and decision makers arrange and rearrange themselves. In the course of these arrangements the meaning of a choice can change several times – if the 'meaning' of a choice is understood as the mix of problems that are discussed in the context of that choice.

Problems are often solved, but rarely by the choice to which they are first attached. A choice that might, under some circumstances, be made with little effort becomes an arena for many problems. As a result, it becomes almost impossible to make, until the problems drift off to another arena. The matching of problems, choices and decision makers is partly controlled by content, 'relevance' and competence; but it is also quite sensitive to timing, the particular combinations of current garbage cans, and the overall load on the system.

[. . .]

Conclusion

We have tried to translate a set of observations made in the study of some university organizations into a model of decision making in what we have called organized anarchies – that is, in situations which do not meet the conditions for more classical models of decision making in some or all of three important ways: preferences are problematic, technology is unclear, or participation is fluid. The garbage can process, as it has been observed, is one in which problems, solutions and participants move from one choice opportunity to another in such a way that the nature of the choice, the time it takes and the problems it solves all depend on a relatively complicated intermeshing of the mix of choices available at any one time, the mix of problems that have access to the organization, the mix of solutions looking for problems and the outside demands on the decision makers.

A major feature of the garbage can process is the partial decoupling of problems and choices. Although we think of decision making as a process for solving problems, that is often not what happens. Problems are worked upon in the context of some choice, but choices are made only when the shifting combinations of problems, solutions and decision makers happen to make action possible. Quite commonly this is after problems have left a given choice arena or before they have discovered it (decisions by flight or oversight).

[. . .]

We acknowledge immediately that no real system can be fully characterized in this way. None the less, the simulated organizations exhibit behaviors that can be observed some of the time in almost all organizations and frequently in some, such as universities. The garbage can model is a possible step toward seeing the systematic interrelatedness of organizational phenomena that are familiar, even common, but that have generally been regarded as isolated and pathological. Measured against a conventional normative model of rational choice, the garbage can process does seem pathological, but such standards are not really appropriate, because the process occurs precisely when the preconditions of more 'normal' rational models are not met.

It is clear that the garbage can process does not do a particularly good job of resolving problems. But it does enable choices to be made and problems sometimes to be resolved even when the organization is plagued with goal ambiguity and conflict, with poorly understood problems that wander in and out of the system, with a variable environment, and with decision makers who may have other things on their minds. This is no mean achievement.

We would argue that there is a large class of significant situations within universities in which the preconditions of the garbage can process probably cannot be eliminated. Indeed, in some, such as pure research, they should not be eliminated. The great advantage of trying to see garbage can phenomena together as a process is the possibility that that process can be understood, that organization design and decision making can take account of its existence, and that, to some extent, it can be managed.

Reference

Cohen, M. D., March, J. G. and Olsen, J. P. (1972). 'A garbage can model of organizational choice'. *Administrative Science Quarterly*, **17**(1), 1–25.

11

Educational organizations as loosely coupled systems

Karl E. Weick

[. . .]

Imagine that you are either the referee, coach, player or spectator at an unconventional soccer match: the field for the game is round; there are several goals scattered haphazardly around the circular field; people can enter and leave the game whenever they want to; they can throw balls in whenever they want; they can say 'that's my goal' whenever they want to, as many times as they want to, and for as many goals as they want to; the entire game takes place on a sloped field; and the game is played as if it makes sense (March, personal communication).

If you now substitute in that example principals for referees, teachers for coaches, students for players, parents for spectators and schooling for soccer, you have an equally unconventional depiction of school organizations. The beauty of this depiction is that it captures a different set of realities within educational organizations than are caught when these same organizations are viewed through the tenets of bureaucratic theory.

Consider the contrast in images. For some time people who manage organizations and people who study this managing have asked, 'How does an organization go about doing what it does and with what consequences for its people, processes, products and persistence?' And for some time they have heard the same answers. In paraphrase the answers say essentially that an organization does what it does because of plans, intentional selection of means that get the organization to agree upon goals, and all of this is accomplished by such rationalized procedures as cost–benefit analyses, division of labor, specified areas of discretion, authority invested in the office, job descriptions, and a consistent evaluation and reward system. The only problem with that portrait is that it is rare in nature. People in organizations, including educational organizations, find themselves hard-pressed either to find actual instances of those rational practices or to find rationalized practices whose outcomes have been as beneficent as predicted, or to feel that those rational occasions explain much of what goes on within the organization. Parts of some organizations are heavily rationalized but many parts also prove intractable to analysis through rational assumptions.

It is this substantial unexplained remainder that is the focus of this chapter. Several people in education have expressed dissatisfaction with the prevailing ideas about organizations supplied by organizational theorists. Fortunately, they have also made some provocative suggestions about newer, more unconventional ideas about organizations that should be given serious thought. A good example of this is the following observation by John M. Stephens (1967, pp. 9–11):

> [There is a] remarkable constancy of educational results in the face of widely differing deliberate approaches. Every so often we adopt new approaches or new methodologies and place our reliance on new panaceas. At the very least we seem to chorus new slogans. Yet the academic growth within the classroom continues at about the same rate, stubbornly refusing to cooperate with the bright new dicta emanating from the conference room. . . . [These observations suggest that] we would be making a great mistake in regarding the management of schools as similar to the process of constructing a building or operating a factory. In these latter processes deliberate decisions play a crucial part, and the enterprise advances or stands still in proportion to the amount of deliberate effort exerted. If we must use a metaphor or model in seeking to understand the process of schooling, we should look to agriculture rather than to the factory. In agriculture we do not start from scratch, and we do not direct our efforts to inert and passive materials. We start, on the contrary, with a complex and ancient process, and we organize our efforts around what seeds, plants, and insects are likely to do anyway. . . . The crop, once planted, may undergo some development even while the farmer sleeps or loafs. No matter what he does, *some* aspects of the outcome will remain constant. When teachers and pupils foregather, some education may proceed even while the Superintendent disports himself in Atlantic City.

It is crucial to highlight what is important in the examples of soccer and schooling viewed as agriculture. To view these examples negatively and dismiss them by observing that 'the referee should tighten up those rules', 'superintendents don't do that', 'schools are more sensible than that', or 'these are terribly sloppy organizations' is to miss the point. The point is although researchers do not know what these kinds of structures are like, [. . .] researchers do know they exist and that each of the negative judgements expressed above makes sense only if the observer assumes that organizations are constructed and managed according to rational assumptions and therefore are scrutable only when rational analyses are applied to them. This chapter attempts to expand and enrich the set of ideas available to people when they try to make sense out of their organizational life. From this standpoint, it is unproductive to observe that fluid participation in schools and soccer is absurd. But it can be more interesting and productive to ask, how can it be that even though the activities in both situations are only modestly connected, the situations are still recognizable and nameable? The goals, player movements and trajectory of the ball are still recognizable and can be labeled 'soccer'. And despite variations in class size, format, locations and architecture, the results are still recognized and can be labeled 'schools'. How can such loose assemblages retain sufficient similarity and permanence across time that they can be recognized, labeled and dealt with? The prevailing ideas in organization theory do not shed much light on how such 'soft' structures develop, persist and impose crude orderliness among their elements.

The basic premise here is that concepts such as loose coupling serve as sensitizing devices. They sensitize the observer to notice and question things that had previously been taken for granted. It is the intent of the program described here to develop a language for use in analyzing complex organizations, a language that may highlight features that have previously gone unnoticed. The guiding principle is a reversal of the common assertion, 'I'll believe it when I see it' and presumes an epistemology that asserts, 'I'll see it when I believe it.' Organizations as loosely coupled systems may not have been seen before because nobody believed in them or could afford to believe in them. It is conceivable that preoccupation with rationalized, tidy, efficient, co-ordinated structures has blinded many practitioners as well as researchers to some of the attractive and unexpected properties of less rationalized and less tightly related clusters of events. This chapter intends to eliminate such blindspots.

The concept of coupling

The phrase 'loose coupling' has appeared in the literature (Glassman, 1973; March and Olsen, 1975) and it is important to highlight the connotation that is captured by this phrase and by no other. It might seem that the word coupling is synonymous with words like connection, link or interdependence, yet each of these latter terms misses a crucial nuance.

By loose coupling, the author intends to convey the image that coupled events are responsive, *but* that each event also preserves its own identity and some evidence of its physical or logical separateness. Thus, in the case of an educational organization, it may be the case that the counselor's office is loosely coupled to the principal's office. The image is that the principal and the counselor are somehow attached, but that each retains some identity and separateness and that their attachment may be circumscribed, infrequent, weak in its mutual effects, unimportant, and/or slow to respond. Each of these connotations would be conveyed if the qualifier loosely were attached

to the word coupled. Loose coupling also carries connotations of imper-
manence, dissolvability and tacitness, all of which are potentially crucial
properties of the 'glue' that holds organizations together.

Glassman (1973) categorizes the degree of coupling between two
systems on the basis of the activity of the variables which the two systems
share. To the extent that two systems either have few variables in common or
share weak variables, they are independent of each other. Applied to the
educational situation, if the principal–vice-principal–superintendent is regarded as one system and the teacher–classroom–pupil–parent–curriculum
as another system, then by Glassman's argument, if we did not find many
variables in the teacher's world to be shared in the world of a principal and/or
if the variables held in common were unimportant relative to the other
variables, then the principal can be regarded as being loosely coupled with the
teacher.

A final advantage of coupling imagery is that it suggests the idea of
building blocks that can be grafted on to an organization or severed with
relatively little disturbance to either the blocks or the organization. Simon
(1969) has argued for the attractiveness of this feature in that most complex
systems can be decomposed into stable sub-assemblies and that these are the
crucial elements in any organization or system. Thus, the coupling imagery
gives researchers access to one of the more powerful ways of talking about
complexity now available.

But if the concept of loose coupling highlights novel images heretofore
unseen in organizational theory, what is it about these images that is worth
seeing?

Coupled elements

There is no shortage of potential coupling elements, but neither is the
population infinite.

At the outset, the two most commonly discussed coupling mechanisms
are the technical core of the organization and the authority of office. The
relevance of these two mechanisms for the issue of identifying elements is that
in the case of technical couplings, each element is some kind of technology,
task, sub-task, role, territory and person, and the couplings are task-induced.
In the case of authority as the coupling mechanism, the elements include
positions, offices, responsibilities, opportunities, rewards and sanctions, and
it is the couplings among these elements that presumably hold the organization together. A compelling argument can be made that *neither* of
these coupling mechanisms is prominent in educational organizations found
in the United States. This leaves one with the question what *does* hold an
educational organization together?

A short list of potential elements in educational organizations will
provide background for subsequent propositions. March and Olsen (1975)

utilize the elements of intention and action. There is a developing position in psychology which argues that intentions are a poor guide for action, intentions often follow rather than precede action, and that intentions and action are loosely coupled. Unfortunately, organizations continue to think that planning is a good thing, they spend much time on planning, and actions are assessed in terms of their fit with plans. Given a potential loose coupling between the intentions and actions of organizational members, it should come as no surprise that administrators are baffled and angered when things never happen the way they were supposed to.

Additional elements may consist of events like yesterday and tomorrow (what happened yesterday may be tightly or loosely coupled with what happens tomorrow) or hierarchical positions like top and bottom, line and staff, or administrators and teachers. An interesting set of elements that lends itself to the loose coupling imagery is means and ends. Frequently, several different means lead to the same outcome. When this happens, it can be argued that any one means is loosely coupled to the end in the sense that there are alternative pathways to achieve that same end. Other elements that might be found in loosely coupled educational systems are teachers–materials, voters–school board, administrators–classroom, process–outcome, teacher–teacher, parent–teacher and teacher–pupil.

While all of these elements are obvious, it is not a trivial matter to specify which elements are coupled. As the concept of coupling is crucial because of its ability to highlight the identity and separateness of elements that are momentarily attached, that conceptual asset puts pressure on the investigator to specify clearly the identity, separateness and boundaries of the elements coupled. While there is some danger of reification when that kind of pressure is exerted, there is the even greater danger of portraying organizations in inappropriate terms which suggest an excess of unity, integration, co-ordination and consensus. If one is non-specific about boundaries in defining elements then it is easy – and careless – to assemble these ill-defined elements and talk about integrated organizations. It is not a trivial issue explaining how elements persevere over time. Weick (1974, pp. 363–4), for example, has argued that elements may appear or disappear and may merge or become separated in response to need–deprivations within the individual, group and/or organization. This means that specification of elements is not a one-shot activity. Given the context of most organizations, elements both appear and disappear over time. For this reason a theory of how elements become loosely or tightly coupled may also have to take account of the fact that the nature and intensity of the coupling may itself serve to create or dissolve elements.

The question of what is available for coupling and decoupling within an organization is an eminently practical question for anyone wishing to have some leverage on a system.

Strength of coupling

Obviously, there is no shortage of meanings for the phrase loose coupling. Researchers need to be clear in their own thinking about whether the phenomenon they are studying is described by two words or three. A researcher can study 'loose coupling' in educational organizations or 'loosely coupled systems'. The shorter phrase, 'loose coupling', simply connotes things, 'any things', that may be tied together either weakly or infrequently or slowly or with minimal interdependence. Whether those things that are loosely coupled exist in a system is of minor importance. Most discussions in this chapter concern loosely coupled systems rather than loose coupling because it wishes to clarify the concepts involved in the perseverance of sets of elements across time.

The idea of loose coupling is evoked when people have a variety of situations in mind. For example, when people describe loosely coupled systems, they are often referring to:

1 Slack times – times when there is an excessive amount of resources relative to demands.
2 Occasions when any one of several means will produce the same end.
3 Richly connected networks in which influence is slow to spread and/or is weak while spreading.
4 A relative lack of co-ordination, slow co-ordination or co-ordination that is dampened as it moves through a system.
5 A relative absence of regulations.
6 Planned unresponsiveness.
7 Actual causal independence.
8 Poor observational capabilities on the part of a viewer.
9 Infrequent inspection of activities within the system.
10 Decentralization.
11 Delegation of discretion.
12 The absence of linkages that should be present based on some theory, e.g. in educational organizations the expected feedback linkage from outcome back to inputs is often non-existent.
13 The observation that an organization's structure is not coterminous with its activity.
14 Those occasions when no matter what you do things always come out the same, e.g. despite all kinds of changes in curriculum, materials, groupings, and so forth, the outcomes in an educational situation remain the same.
15 Curricula or courses in educational organizations for which there are few prerequisites, i.e. the longer the string of prerequisites, the tighter the coupling.

Potential functions and dysfunctions of loose coupling

It is important to note that the concept of loose coupling need not be used normatively. People who are steeped in the conventional literature of organizations may regard loose coupling as a sin or something to be apologized for. This chapter takes a neutral, if not mildly affectionate, stance toward the concept. Apart from whatever effect one might feel toward the idea of loose coupling, it does appear *a priori* that certain functions can be served by having a system in which the elements are loosely coupled. Below are listed seven potential functions that could be associated with loose coupling plus additional reasons why each advantage might also be a liability. The dialectic generated by each of these oppositions begins to suggest dependent variables that should be sensitive to variations in the tightness of coupling.

1 The basic argument of Glassman (1973) is that loose coupling allows some portions of an organization to persist. Loose coupling lowers the probability that the organization will have to – or be able to – respond to each little change in the environment that occurs. The mechanism of voting, for example, allows elected officials to remain in office for a full term even though their constituency at any moment may disapprove of particular actions. Some identity and separateness of the element 'elected official' is preserved relative to a second element, 'constituency', by the fact of loosely coupled accountability which is measured in 2-, 4- or 6-year terms. While loose coupling may foster perseverance, it is not selective in what is perpetuated. Thus archaic traditions as well as innovative improvizations may be perpetuated.

2 A second advantage of loose coupling is that it may provide a sensitive sensing mechanism. This possibility is suggested by Fritz Heider's perceptual theory of things and medium. Heider (1959) argues that perception is most accurate when a medium senses a thing and the medium contains many independent elements that can be externally constrained. When elements in a medium become either fewer in number and/or more internally constrained and/or more interdependent, their ability to represent some remote thing is decreased. Thus sand is a better medium to display wind currents than are rocks, the reason being that sand has more elements, more independence among the elements, and the elements are subject to a greater amount of external constraint than is the case for rocks. Using Heider's formulation metaphorically, it could be argued that loosely coupled systems preserve many independent sensing elements and therefore 'know' their environments better than is true for more tightly coupled systems which have fewer externally constrained, independent elements. Balanced against this improvement in sensing is the possibility that the system would become increasingly vulnerable to producing faddish responses and interpretations. If the environment is known better, then this could induce more frequent changes in activities done in response to this 'superior intelligence'.

3 A loosely coupled system may be a good system for localized adaptation. If all of the elements in a large system are loosely coupled to one another, then any one element can adjust to and modify a local unique contingency without affecting the whole system. These local adaptations can be swift, relatively economical and substantial. By definition, the antithesis of localized adaptation is standardization and to the extent that standardization can be shown to be desirable, a loosely coupled system might exhibit fewer of these presumed benefits. For example, the localized adaptation characteristic of loosely coupled systems may result in a lessening of educational democracy.

4 In loosely coupled systems where the identity, uniqueness and separateness of elements is preserved, the system potentially can retain a greater number of mutations and novel solutions than would be the case with a tightly coupled system. A loosely coupled system could preserve more 'cultural insurance' to be drawn upon in times of radical change than is the case for more tightly coupled systems. Loosely coupled systems may be elegant solutions to the problem that adaptation can preclude adaptability. When a specific system fits into an ecological niche and does so with great success, this adaptation can be costly. It can be costly because resources which are useless in a current environment might deteriorate or disappear even though they could be crucial in a modified environment. It is conceivable that loosely coupled systems preserve more diversity in responding than do tightly coupled systems, and therefore can adapt to a considerably wider range of changes in the environment than would be true for tightly coupled systems. To appreciate the possible problems associated with this abundance of mutations, reconsider the dynamic outlined in the preceding discussion of localized adaptation. If a local set of elements can adapt to local idiosyncrasies without involving the whole system, then this same loose coupling could also forestall the spread of advantageous mutations that exist somewhere in the system. While the system may contain novel solutions for new problems of adaptation, the very structure that allows these mutations to flourish may prevent their diffusion.

5 If there is a breakdown in one portion of a loosely coupled system then this breakdown is sealed off and does not affect other portions of the organization. Previously, we had noted that loosely coupled systems are an exquisite mechanism to adapt swiftly to local novelties and unique problems. Now we are carrying the analysis one step further, and arguing that when any element misfires or decays or deteriorates, the spread of this deterioration is checked in a loosely coupled system. While this point is reminiscent of earlier functions, the emphasis here is on the localization of trouble rather than the localization of adaptation. But even this potential benefit may be problematic. A loosely coupled system can isolate its trouble spots and prevent the trouble from spreading, but it should be difficult for the loosely coupled system to repair the defective element. If weak influences pass from the defective portions to the functioning

portions, then the influence back from these functioning portions will also be weak and probably too little, too late.

6 Because some of the most important elements in educational organizations are teachers, classrooms, principals, and so forth, it may be consequential that in a loosely coupled system there is more room available for self-determination by the actors. If it is argued that a sense of efficacy is crucial for human beings, then a sense of efficacy might be greater in a loosely coupled system with autonomous units than it would be in a tightly coupled system where discretion is limited. A further comment can be made about self-determination to provide an example of the kind of imagery that is invoked by the concept of loose coupling.

It is possible that much of the teacher's sense of – and actual – control comes from the fact that diverse interested parties expect the teacher to link their intentions with teaching actions. Such linking of diverse intentions with actual work probably involves considerable negotiation. A parent complains about a teacher's action and the teacher merely points out to the parent how the actions are really correspondent with the parent's desires for the education of his or her children. Because most actions have ambiguous consequences, it should always be possible to justify the action as fitting the intentions of those who complain. Salancik (1975) goes even further and suggests the intriguing possibility that when the consequences of an action are ambiguous, the stated *intentions* of the action serve as surrogates for the consequences. Because it is not known whether reading a certain book is good or bad for a child, the fact that it is intended to be good for the child itself becomes justification for having the child read it. The potential trade-off implicit in this function of loose coupling is fascinating. There is an increase in autonomy in the sense that resistance is heightened, but this heightened resistance occurs at the price of shortening the chain of consequences that will flow from each autonomous actor's efforts. Each teacher will have to negotiate separately with the same complaining parent.

7 A loosely coupled system should be relatively inexpensive to run because it takes time and money to co-ordinate people. As much of what happens and should happen inside educational organizations seems to be defined and validated outside the organization, schools are in the business of building and maintaining categories, a business that requires co-ordination only on a few specific issues, e.g. assignment of teachers. This reduction in the necessity for co-ordination results in fewer conflicts, fewer inconsistencies among activities, fewer discrepancies between categories and activity. Thus, loosely coupled systems seem to hold the costs of co-ordination to a minimum. Despite this being an inexpensive system, loose coupling is also a non-rational system of fund allocation and, therefore, unspecifiable, unmodifiable, and incapable of being used as means of change.

When these several sets of functions and dysfunctions are examined, they begin to throw several research issues into relief. For example, oppositions proposed in each of the preceding seven points suggest the importance of contextual theories. A predicted outcome or its opposite should emerge depending on how and in what the loosely coupled system is embedded. The preceding oppositions also suggest a fairly self-contained research program. Suppose a researcher starts with the first point made – as loose coupling increases the system should contain a greater number of anachronistic practices. Loosely coupled systems should be conspicuous for their cultural lags. Initially, one would like to know whether that is plausible or not. But then one would want to examine in more fine-grained detail whether those anachronistic practices that are retained hinder the system or impose structure and absorb uncertainty, thereby producing certain economies in responding. Similar embellishment and elaboration is possible for each function with the result that rich networks of propositions become visible. What is especially attractive about these networks is that there is little precedent for them in the organizational literature. Despite this, these propositions contain a great deal of face validity when they are used as filters to look at educational organizations. When compared, for example, with the bureaucratic template mentioned in the introduction, the template associated with loosely coupled systems seems to take the observer into more interesting territory and prods him or her to ask more interesting questions.

   [. . .]

Conclusion: A statement of priorities

More time should be spent examining the possibility that educational organizations are most usefully viewed as loosely coupled systems. The concept of organizations as loosely coupled systems can have a substantial effect on existing perspectives about organizations. To probe further into the plausibility of that assertion, it is suggested that the following research priorities constitute a reasonable approach to the examination of loosely coupled systems.

1. Develop conceptual tools capable of preserving loosely coupled systems

It is clear that more conceptual work has to be done before other lines of inquiry on this topic are launched. Much of the blandness in organizational theory these days can be traced to investigators applying impoverished images to organizational settings. If researchers immediately start stalking the elusive loosely coupled system with imperfect language and concepts, they will perpetuate the blandness of organizational theory.

   [. . .]

2. Explicate what elements are available in educational organizations for coupling

This activity has high priority because it is essential to know the practical domain within which the coupling phenomena occur. Because there is the further complication that elements may appear or disappear as a function of context and time, this type of inventory is essential at an early stage of inquiry. An indirect benefit of making this a high priority activity is that it will stem the counterproductive suspicion that 'the number of elements in educational organizations is infinite'. The reasonable reply to that comment is that if one is precise in defining and drawing boundaries around elements, then the number of elements will be less than imagined. Furthermore, the researcher can reduce the number of relevant elements if he has some theoretical ideas in mind. These theoretical ideas should be one of the outcomes of initial activity devoted to language and concept development (Priority 1).

3. Develop contextual methodology

Given favourable outcomes from the preceding two steps, researchers should then be eager to look at complex issues such as patterns of tight and loose coupling keeping in mind that loose coupling creates major problems for the researcher because he is trained and equipped to decipher predictable, tightly coupled worlds. To 'see' loosely coupled worlds, unconventional methodologies need to be developed and conventional methodologies that are under-exploited need to be given more attention. Among the existing tools that should be refined to study loose coupling are comparative studies and longitudinal studies. Among the new tools that should be 'invented' because of their potential relevance to loosely coupled systems are non-teleological thinking (Steinbeck, 1941), concurrence methodology (Bateson, 1972, pp. 180–201), and Hegelian, Kantian and Singerian inquiring systems (Mitroff, 1974). While these latter methodologies are unconventional within social science, so too is it unconventional to urge that we treat unpredictability (loose coupling) as our topic of interest rather than a nuisance.

4. Promote the collection of thorough, concrete descriptions of the coupling patterns in actual educational organizations

No descriptive studies are available to show what couplings in what patterns and with what strengths exist in current educational organizations. This oversight should be remedied as soon as possible.

Adequate descriptions should be of great interest to the practitioner who wants to know how his influence attempts will spread and with what intensity. Adequate description should also show practitioners how their organizations may be more sensible and adaptive than they suspect. Thorough descriptions of coupling should show checks and balances, localized controls, stabilizing mechanisms and subtle feedback loops that keep the organization stable and that would promote its decay if they were tampered with.

The benefits for the researcher of full descriptions are that they would suggest which locations and which questions about loose coupling are most likely to explain sizeable portions of the variance in organizational outcomes. For example, on the basis of good descriptive work, it might be found that both tightly and loosely coupled systems 'know' their environments with equal accuracy, in which case, the earlier line of theorizing about 'thing and medium' would be given a lower priority.

5. *Specify the nature of core technology in educational organizations*

A surprisingly large number of the ideas presented in this chapter assume that the typical coupling mechanisms of authority of office and logic of the task do not operate in educational organizations. Inquiry into loosely coupled systems was triggered partly by efforts to discover what *does* accomplish the coupling in school systems. Before the investigation of loose coupling goes too far, it should be established that authority and task are not prominent coupling mechanisms in schools. The assertions that they are not prominent seem to issue from a combination of informal observation, implausibility, wishful thinking, looking at the wrong things, and rather vague definitions of core technology and reward structures within education. If these two coupling mechanisms were defined clearly, studied carefully and found to be weak and/or non-existent in schools, *then* there would be a powerful justification for proceeding vigorously to study loosely coupled systems. Given the absence of work that definitively discounts these coupling mechanisms in education and given the fact that these two mechanisms have accounted for much of the observed couplings in other kinds of organizations, it seems crucial to look for them in educational organizations in the interest of parsimony.

It should be emphasized that if it *is* found that substantial coupling within educational organizations is due to authority of office and logic of the task, this does not negate the agenda that is sketched out in this chapter. Instead, such discoveries would (1) make it even more crucial to look for patterns of coupling to explain outcomes, (2) focus attention on tight and loose couplings within task- and authority-induced couplings, (3) alert researchers to keep close watch for any coupling mechanisms other than these two, and (4) would direct comparative research toward settings in which these two coupling mechanisms vary in strength and form. ·

6. *Probe empirically the ratio of functions to dysfunctions associated with loose coupling*

Although the word 'function' has had a checkered history, it is used here without apology – and without the surplus meanings and ideology that have become attached to it. Earlier, several potential benefits of loose coupling were described and these descriptions were balanced by additional suggestions of potential liabilities. If one adopts an evolutionary epistemology, then over time one expects that entities develop a more exquisite fit with their ecological niches. Given that assumption, one then argues that if loosely coupled systems exist and if they have existed for sometime, then they bestow some net advantage to their inhabitants and/or their constituencies. It is not obvious, however, what these advantages are. A set of studies showing how schools benefit and suffer given their structure as loosely coupled systems should do much to improve the quality of thinking devoted to organizational analysis.

7. Discover how inhabitants make sense out of loosely coupled worlds

Scientists are going to have some big problems when their topic of inquiry becomes low probability couplings, but just as scientists have special problems comprehending loosely coupled worlds, so too must the inhabitants of these worlds. It would seem that quite early in a research program on loose coupling, examination of this question should be started as it has direct relevance to those practitioners who must thread their way through such 'invisible' worlds and must concern their sense-making and stories in such a way that they do not bump into each other while doing so.

[. . .]

References

Bateson, M. C. (1972). *Our Own Metaphor*. New York: Knopf.
Glassman, R. B. (1973). 'Persistence and Loose Coupling in Living Systems'. *Behavioral Science*, **18**, 83–98.
Heider, F. (1959). 'Thing and Medium'. *Psychological Issues*, **1**(3), 1–34.
March, J. G. and Olsen, J. P. (1975). 'Choice Situations in Loosely Coupled Worlds'. Unpublished manuscript, Stanford University.
Mitroff, I. I. (1974). *The Subjective Side of Science*. New York: Elsevier.
Salancik, G. R. (1975). 'Notes on Loose Coupling: Linking Intentions to Actions'. Unpublished manuscript, University of Illinois.
Simon, H. A. (1969). 'The Architecture of Complexity'. *Proceedings of the American Philosophical Society*, **106**, 467–82.
Steinbeck, J. (1941). *The Log from the Sea of Cortez*. New York: Viking.
Stephens, J. M. (1967). *The Process of Schooling*. New York: Holt, Rinehart and Winston.
Weick, K. E. (1974). 'Middle Range Theories of Social Systems'. *Behavioral Science*, **19**, 357–67.

12

Ambiguity models and secondary schools: A case study*

Les Bell

Rational models of organizations such as Weber's work on bureaucracy (see Chapter 2) attribute to schools orderliness, rationality and predictability within which office holders apply agreed rules and procedures in a consistent, impartial manner. By implication it is thought that the membership of the school can easily be identified and the boundaries clearly defined. It is assumed that the relationship between members is clear for achieving desired goals. Relationships with the external environment tend to be stable and predictable, or, where this is not the case, can be coped with by the application of the relevant rules and procedures. On the evidence derived from this type of analysis an observer might expect, for example, that decisions formulated in schools would be the result of a logical and rational process in which those eligible to participate did so, and that the importance of the decision to be taken would be determined by the priority attributed to it by the potential decision makers. In fact, this view is, in some ways, positively misleading, as it is predicated on the assumption that schools have more control over such factors as the environment within which they operate, and decision-taking, than is often the case. Schools frequently have to react to decisions taken elsewhere over which they have little or no influence. Decisions that are made within schools are often constrained by external factors over which they have no control. Falling pupil numbers, changes in school staffing levels and, more recently, the proposals contained within the Education Reform Act, are all examples of matters external to schools, and beyond their power to control or influence, that

*The research upon which this chapter is based was funded by a grant from the Nuffield Foundation, who are also funding continued research at Oakfields. I am grateful for their support. I am also grateful for the support, cooperation and encouragement given to me by the headteacher and staff of the school.

make rational planning and decision making within schools difficult to achieve. Thus schools operate in a complex and unstable environment over which they can exert only modest control and which is capable of producing effects which penetrate the strongest and most selective of boundaries (Bell, 1980). Schools are not able to disregard these pressures within their wider environment, nor are they able to respond to the uncertainty which such pressures bring by attempting to buffer themselves against the unforeseen or by gaining control over the source of the uncertainty. Schools in such situations tend to display many of the features attributed by Cohen and March (1974) to ambiguous organizations.

In this chapter it is intended to explore the impact of a turbulent environment upon one school. Three features of the school's organization – its goals, technology and membership – will be examined in order to establish how far the school's inability to control the pressures emanating from its wider environment produced the effects anticipated by Cohen and March. They suggest, in Chapter 10 of this volume, that such environmental turbulence will result in a situation in which the goals of the school are unclear, the technology used within the school is inadequately understood, and the membership of the school is fluid. This school owed its very existence to environmental turbulence. It was formed in 1985 by the amalgamation of two single-sex bilateral schools occupying the same campus but with *distinct and separate* existences. A third school, a 12–16 secondary modern school, that occupied a site about a mile away, was also involved. The amalgamation was part of a strategy developed by the Local Education Authority (LEA) to cope with declining pupil numbers. It was opposed by the staff, parents and pupils of the secondary modern school and by groups associated with the other two schools. Opposition to the amalgamations in the boys' school intensified when the headmistress of the girls' school was appointed headteacher of the new school.

The environment which produced this school can be seen, therefore, to be turbulent in many different ways. For much of the period during which preparations were being made for the amalgamation, constraints were imposed on those processes by teachers' union action that precluded staff from attending meetings out of the normal school day. This severely inhibited much of the forward planning that was necessary. It also meant that some teachers believed that they were ill-informed about what was going on and that others felt divided loyalties between their school and their union. From the outset of negotiations it was obvious that all three schools were going to suffer extensively from falling pupil numbers. It was also clear that the strategies to be adopted by the LEA in the future could not leave the newly formed school untouched. Throughout the negotiations over merger, many of those involved were conscious that the new school would have to shed substantial numbers of staff over the first 5 years of its existence. It was also possible that the school would have its sixth form removed. Amalgamation tended to be viewed by the participants as a stage in a process of contraction rather than as a once-and-for-all change. Furthermore, the amalgamation had been initiated outside the three schools as a result of political responses to demographic changes. The whole process was a result of environmental turbulence external to the school. It was clear that the staff of the new school would be able to exert very little influence over policy decisions that might fundamentally change the nature of the institution in which they worked. Perhaps because of this feeling of powerlessness among some sections of the staff, many of the tensions that had surrounded the struggle over the amalgamation were still in evidence as the school opened. More probable, however, the events that took place in the early weeks of the school's existence can be explained by three further factors. These are the extent to which teachers felt loyalty to and identification with their previous schools; the way in which the processes of appointing staff had been carried out in the months before the amalgamation; and the reactions of different groups to the ways in which the headteacher and her senior management team set about the tasks of managing the new school.

The new school, Oakfields, was a bilateral school with some 1500 pupils on roll in September 1985. This number was expected to fall to about 900 by 1990. On opening it was a split-site school, the facilities of the secondary modern school being retained for use with pupils in their final year at that school as a result of a promise given by the area education officer to the parents of those pupils during the merger negotiations. The school admits all of its pupils at 12+, some as a result of selection tests and others who are drawn from the catchment area. Students who choose to stay on at the sixth form are joined by others from nearby high schools.

There were approximately 85 teachers on the staff, including part-timers. The actual figure was difficult to determine at any one time because of the extremely flexible use made in the school of part-time staff. This chapter is based on intensive interviews with 53 members of staff. All staff were offered the opportunity of interview. Only ten declined outright, although four of them provided written evidence. Three others were ill during most of the period of the interviews. Of the remainder, five were new to the school and seven were part-time teachers who felt that they had little to say about the merger process. The difficulties of timetabling and of providing cover prevented the other interviews taking place. Each of the three deputy headteachers and one of the two senior teachers was interviewed three times. The headteacher was interviewed five times over a period of 18 months including one interview after she had taken up another appointment. The LEA officer responsible for the school was also interviewed. A questionnaire was distributed to all staff which gave them the opportunity to express their opinions and to allow those who had been interviewed to give any further information that they thought to be relevant. The response rate was 45%, although 25 teachers indicated that they felt they had covered all that they wanted to say in the interview with the researcher.

This chapter is an exploration of the ways in which the staff of Oakfields School responded to and made sense of the environmental turbulence that characterized their situation in the early days following the opening of the school.

The aims of the school

In times of change schools display those characteristics described by Cohen and March (1974) as organizational ambiguities. In such situations it may not be at all clear what the goals of the school are. Different members of the school may perceive different goals, attribute different priorities to the same goals, or even be unable to define goals which have any operational meaning. Thus while it is commonly expected that those who work in schools should have some overall purpose it is likely that the organizational context of many schools actually renders this either impossible or very difficult. Hence schools face an ambiguity of purpose, the result of which is that the achievement of goals which are educational in any real sense cease to be central to the functioning of the school. Thus uncertainty generated by falling pupil numbers, school closure and merger, and the need to cope with such changes overshadow much of the work done with existing pupils. A common sense of direction is frequently not evident in the teaching which does take place. Furthermore, it has often been found difficult to specify a constant set of educational goals. They have tended to change over time and may even vary between different parts of the school organization. They are frequently stated in terms which are notoriously difficult to translate into action and, while goals may be imputed to schools by observing the behaviour of a range of people within them, this imputation itself tends to be as ambiguous as the goals, because it is extremely difficult to obtain general agreement on it.

At Oakfields School it was possible to identify a series of statements about the common purpose of the school. In a document called 'What the School will be About', produced by the head very soon after her appointment in 1985 and circulated to all staff, she made it clear that if anything was to be achieved in Oakfields then it was essential that everyone knew what the goals of the school were and how they were to be achieved. The goals of the school were: to enlarge a child's knowledge, experience and imaginative understanding and thus develop an awareness of moral values and the capacity for enjoyment; and to enable children to enter the world after formal education as an active participant in society and a responsible contributor to it, capable of achieving as much independence as possible. The first priority was to create a school where all its members were treated with equal respect and where the emphasis was on creating a happy, challenging atmosphere conducive to the development of those characteristics that had been identified as being part of the aims of the school. The head pointed out that the [. . .] school was, first and foremost, a place for the children. She concluded by saying that how this was to be achieved was open for all the staff to discuss in the coming months.

It appears, therefore, that the head identified the goals, although the means of operationalizing them was as yet undecided or, at best, unclear. Within a few weeks of the school opening the head reminded her staff that a school could only function well when everyone pulled in the same direction, the implication being that this was not happening. She further pointed out to the staff that they had to recognize that they were now all one school and that this would become evident in all that they did. She acknowledged that the aims of the school did not find universal acceptance among her colleagues when she wrote, in the same document:

> You may not agree with some of the policies and procedures or even with the long term aims, but until we can discuss these I should like everyone to enforce them for all our sakes, but especially for the good of the children.

In a later document the aims were somewhat reinterpreted. They were summarized as being to create an effective learning environment. The difficulties of achieving them were recognized after a school-wide exercise, carried out by senior staff, on following groups of pupils throughout a teaching day. The head argued that it was necessary to return to basic principles to decide what skills, attitudes and knowledge the pupils needed, and that the staff had to decide how to present these so that the pupils could relate one area of learning with another. Again she appealed to the staff to accept and implement school policy as it was laid down in the 'What the School will be About' document. It was evident that the school had not solved the problem of operationalizing its goals. This situation can, in part, be explained by the different perceptions that groups of staff held about the new school, about their previous school, and about constituent schools. The perceptions that they brought to the new situation played a large part in determining their responses to it, especially in terms of how far they accepted the aims of Oakfields School and about how far and by what processes they were prepared to set about attempting to operationalize those aims.

Almost all of the staff of Oakfields had a reasonably clear view about the nature of the constituent schools, although the perceived differences were interpreted in a variety of ways. The boys' school was generally regarded as being traditional or formal. Its strengths were identified in terms of examination results and firm discipline both in its approach to its pupils and its internal organization. As one teacher put it, the boys' school was dominated by a few very strong characters at the top. The girls' school placed greater emphasis on self-responsibility on the part of the pupils and it had a stronger pastoral tradition, although its examination results were also very sound. The staff were thought to be more involved in decision making at all levels. The secondary school had a reputation for being a caring school and had established for itself a good reputation in a multicultural area. Its examination success did not compare with the other two schools. Staff from outside the boys' school tended to see it as autocratic and overly rigid with too great a reliance on various forms of punishment. Many of the boys' school staff saw the girls' school staff as lax or soft. The seconday school staff were more of an unknown quantity because that school had been some distance away from the other two. The general view was that they might find some of the academic work rather demanding but they should be good in the pastoral area. It was widely acknowledged that they knew their pupils very well. In some ways these views were stereotypes because it is uncertain whether they were based on any evidence, although the views expressed tended to be shared by the staff from the other two schools.

These perspectives were used by the teachers to make sense of much that was going on in Oakfields and to make judgements about it. For example, it was relatively common to find the staff from the boys' school stating that the discipline in the new school was too lax and that what was required was a firm disciplinarian in the senior management team. There was a fear that, as a result of the appointment of the head of the girls' school to Oakfields, the regime would be too liberal and standards would drop. A criticism frequently made by the girls' school staff of some of their colleagues from the boys' school was that they were unable to develop the necessary skills for fostering self-discipline in their pupils and that their views of how a school should be run were rooted in the past. Such differences in perspective resulted in a number of different interpretations of the stated aims of Oakfields School and of how the rules and procedures should be applied. Should pupils be allowed inside the school at lunchtime and be encouraged to exhibit self-discipline or should they be sent outside, for example? Thus at a school level it was clear that, for some staff, their interpretation of the goals of the new school and their stance towards operationalizing those goals owed as much to their perception of the three constituent schools as it did to any statement of intent from the head of Oakfields. It was also clear that the aims allowed a variety of interpretations such that, in any single instance, a variety of responses might be appropriate.

A similar situation pertained in some, but not all, departments as they prepared to face the opening of the new school. One departmental head was quite clear about the extent to which the different philosophies at school level had an impact on his work. He pointed out that:

> In my own area [in the girls' school] we were following a fairly modern course using texts and work sheets that were designed to make children think. The boys' school were using a traditional text written in the 1950s. The secondary school was somewhere between the two. They were using a set of booklets with slightly more modern presentation.

This head of department attempted to involve his new colleagues in decision taking about appropriate texts by leaving examples in strategic places. One senior colleague refused to look at any material until the new school opened. He continued to use his old material even after that. Others were surprised at being asked to express an opinion and helped to select a new scheme. It proved impossible, however, to provide sufficient resources for all classes to start on the new scheme in September 1985. Although some agreement on the way to implement departmental aims was arrived at, it proved impossible to ensure that these were implemented by all the staff at one and the same time.

In another department a combination of subjects had been deliberately brought together to ensure that the children gained a coherent experience. The headteacher was concerned from the outset that this departmental head might run it as a series of separate subjects. This he succeeded in doing. As one teacher put it: 'The History and Geography areas are going their own ways. I teach Economics but this does not seem to impinge on History and Geography.' No real attempt was being made here to ensure that pupils could see the relationships between one area and another even when those areas came under the same subject area. This was justified on the grounds that early specialization was necessary in order to ensure that the children were successful in public examinations, but this took no account of the experience being given to the children or of possible alternative syllabuses. Here again the school's aims were being interpreted in a way that was contrary to their original intention, as one of the expressed aims of the school was to enable pupils to recognize and understand the interrelationships between subject areas. Thus much of what went on within the school was not consistent with its stated aims.

The technology of the school

Given, then, that in such situations the educational goals are ambiguous and may well not occupy a focal position in school life, the way in which schools attempt to fulfil these goals is equally unclear. Even when the goals are expressed in the most general terms, different educational and political ideologies may lead teachers to approach their tasks in a number of ways. More fundamentally, however, teachers are often unsure about what it is they want their pupils to learn, about what it is the pupils have learned, and how, if at all, learning has actually taken place. The learning process is inadequately understood, and therefore pupils may not always be learning effectively. The basic technology available in schools is often not understood because its purposes are only vaguely recognized. In such a situation teachers do not so much acquire and use the skills of teaching as learn how to conform to the normative and formal structures in order to reduce the demands made upon them by the organization to acceptable proportions. Because the related technology is so unclear the processes of teaching and learning are clouded in ambiguity. This produces a range of situations in which rules and procedures cannot be operated with consistency, impartiality and predict-ability, because the various parties involved do not perceive with any degree of clarity what is expected of others. Thus, although the schools manage to exist as entities their processes are not really understood by their members. They operate on the basis of procedures such as trial and error, learning from the accidents of past experience and pragmatic inventions of necessity.

In her paper outlining the aims of the school the headteacher recognized that translating those aims into actions presented considerable difficulty. In so doing she acknowledged the problems faced by all schools in determining the appropriate relationship between the ends which are identified and the means to be employed to achieve those ends. This is especially true in a school where 'achieving independence' is a stated aim. Much of the technology, in the sense of how things are done, employed in more traditional schools such as the boys' school, tends to lead to the dependence of the pupil on the teacher and of the teacher on the prescribed syllabus rather than producing rela-tionships based on independence and individual autonomy. It is not surpris-ing, given the different backgrounds of the staff, to find that within some departments there was considerable debate about teaching styles and their relative appropriateness for the children of Oakfields. This debate became more intense as some areas of the school moved more towards pupil-directed and participative learning and teaching. The head was forced to remind some of her staff that 'pupils' active involvement in the lesson improves the span of attention considerably and the increase in project work for GCSE will make the 35-minute period quite impracticable.'

The debate about means was not only about teaching style and the content of lessons. It was also about the structuring of the timetable. Here again the dispute focused on how a particular end could and should be achieved. If the end was to teach specific content and skills related to a specified subject area then the debate was about how far that particular subject area needed its own slots on the timetable and where those slots should be. Science subjects were especially adamant that each science had to be time-tabled separately in double periods. One teacher argued strongly that where one group had adjacent periods of Physics and Chemistry, the children would become very confused about the distinction between the different aspects of science. The headteacher, at about the same time, was trying to encourage her staff to ensure that the children saw the connection between different parts of their work.

The debate about means and ends in the science subjects had its parallel in other areas of the school. In Craft, Design and Technology (CDT), and in Humanities, teachers were constantly discussing whether each subject should have a base to which the children came or whether teachers should move to classes. Central to this argument was the issue of how far it was practical for teachers or children to carry all the materials required for particular lessons. At first glance such concerns, common as they are to many schools, appear relatively trivial. Their continued existence, the apparent inability of members of the institution to resolve them, and their very real impact on both teaching and learning indicate, however, that schools, like many other organizations, have a problematic technology in that the means are often not related to serving the needs of the client group, i.e. the children.

Other examples of this lack of specificity in the means–ends relationship abound in Oakfields School. Great emphasis is placed both in public documents and in the rhetoric of the internal debates on the school as a caring institution and as a place where individual personal development will be fostered. Yet the pastoral structure and the resources available to pastoral tutors made the achievement of such aims extremely difficult. Form tutors complained regularly that it was almost impossible to understand where any child was at a particular time of the day, so complex was the timetable. This was summed up by one teacher who, after counselling a very distressed child, let the child return to her lessons. The teacher intended to check later in the morning that the child was feeling better. When the child had gone the teacher realized that she had no way of locating the child.

At the same time those teaching the Personal and Social Development part of pastoral care were unhappy with the materials at their disposal. As one teacher put it, the materials were vague and many of them seemed to be irrelevant to what they should be trying to do. She suggested that perhaps the staff had not been given enough guidance, but even if all staff understood exactly what was required, the resource-based material was not available. She also remarked that some of her colleagues were quite stubborn and that they did not like to change their approach to this aspect of their work, and therefore though some teachers continued to do what they had always done, they claimed to be working towards achieving the espoused aims of the new school. This again shows how problematic the relationship is between means and ends at Oakfields.

The membership of the school

The third major characteristic of ambiguous organizations is that of fluid membership. Membership might be fluid in two senses. First, the school consists of groups of pupils and teachers all of whom make a wide range of demands on the organization. By their very nature schools gain and lose large numbers of pupils each year and, during an amalgamation, large numbers of staff may move or change their roles. This is especially true where there are significant numbers of part-time staff, as was the case at Oakfields. Membership of the school also becomes fluid in the sense that the extent to which individuals are willing and able to participate in its activities may change over time and according to the nature of the activity itself. In this way schools are peopled by participants who wander in and out. The notion of membership is thus ambiguous, and therefore it becomes extremely difficult to attribute responsibility to a particular member of the school for some areas of the school's activities while, over other areas, there exist considerable conflicts of interest.

Within Oakfields School this manifested itself in a number of ways. The first relates directly to pupils and the extent to which they actually acknowledged their own membership of the school. Many of the older pupils of all three constituent schools found it hard to accept they were members of a new institution; they tried in a number of ways to retain the identities of their previous schools. This was especially true of the fifth-year pupils who had previously been at the secondary school. They remained on the same campus, and were not integrated into the new school in any sense except administratively. They even used the name of their old school to describe themselves. This situation was only to last for one year but it had a profound effect on the pupils. It also had a similar effect on many of the teaching staff, especially those who still retained a strong feeling of loyalty to the old school.

Teachers had to travel half a mile or so to the old secondary school campus. This was extremely inconvenient given the problems with time-tabling and 'travelling time'. More important than this, however, was the psychological effect. Those teachers who had previously been members of staff at the secondary school and who found themselves returning there had their old allegiances rekindled. A number of former secondary school staff indicated that they felt that they were second-class citizens in the new school, because of their lack of sixth-form teaching experience and because most of them were non-graduates. They also believed that their very real skills were undervalued and that they were viewed and treated as inferior partners in the merger. Though it was difficult to produce any real evidence for this, several of them noted how difficult it was for them to feel any sense of belonging to the new institution since these feelings existed and when they were constantly going to the old school where the old ethos and much of the old ways of doing things were retained. This was, in fact, the reality for not only were the fifth year pupils still at the school, so was its headmaster who still fulfilled that role in spite of the fact that he was not no longer the headteacher but was designated an associate headteacher, and had little, if any, contact with the main school and, as far as possible, retained all the trappings and the practices of his old school. While this was quite understandable it made the position of those teachers who had been members of his staff extremely delicate. They experienced a conflict of loyalties, not least because much that he retained appeared to be in direct conflict with the new regime. He could only be described as being a member of Oakfields School if the notion of membership is used to indicate the most tenuous of connections. Several of his erstwhile colleagues took up a similar position to the extent that they were in the new school but not of it.

One of these teachers provides us with an extreme example of the second type of fluid participation – that of a teacher who opted to avoid, as far as possible, taking any part in the school's way of doing things or its processes of decision making. Several other teachers in Mathematics, French, Humanities and CDT adopted similar positions. Others concentrated entirely on their own work in the classroom but took little, if any, part in decision making at departmental or the whole-school level. Some teachers decided to avoid, as far as possible, taking part in anything that did not directly relate to their work in the classroom. Others opted into and out of decision-making procedures. Yet others, especially at middle-management level, played a significant part in these processes. Even the senior management team was criticized by many teachers because its members were not regularly seen around the school and did not know the children. The headteacher was more concerned at this stage with making and keeping contact with her staff. The senior management team tended to be concerned with administrative tasks and dealing with day-to-day organization and related problems. This was interpreted by some teachers as not becoming involved in the real tasks of the school in terms of defining appropriate and inappropriate behaviour, enforcing rules and procedures, and identifying with and being identified by other members of the school, including the pupils.

This variation and disagreement over the most appropriate forms of participation can, to some extent, be explained by the union action that was at its height during this period. More than one teacher commented on a feeling of divided loyalties between the union and the school. Such feelings were not confined to those teachers who had previously taught at the secondary school, and the results of the union action were, in the view of the head, to make the life of the new school as difficult as possible by preventing many of the meetings, discussions and other activities that would have enabled decisions to be taken after consultation with the whole or a major part of the staff. These would have helped to foster a feeling of identity and a sense of membership. The senior management team believed that the union action placed additional administrative burdens upon them. In the event, therefore, membership of the school and commitment to its various processes, as far as the teaching staff were concerned, were relatively fluid because of pressures external to the school and factors pertaining to the processes of amalgamation, as well as the variation in commitment to organizational activities which can be found in many institutions.

Decision making in the school

Unclear goals and technology and fluid participation in an organization are crucial elements in determining how an organization takes decisions. They are also significant in determining the nature and quality of the decisions that come to be made and implemented. Decisions taken in such circumstances, and the solutions that become identified with particular problems, are rarely based on some notion of common goals to be achieved or of a rational approach to finding solutions based on a clear view of what is necessary for the school to be managed effectively in conditions of ambiguity. Problem solving is more likely to consist of linking together problems, solutions, participants and choices in relatively random ways because there are no clear criteria against which the quality, rationality or acceptability of decisions can be tested. Even if such criteria do exist, they tend to become submerged under a deluge of other issues, all of which need to be confronted. Hence decision making and problem solving become unpredictable. Unpredictability here refers to the way in which the factors listed above are combined rather than to the long- or short-term feasibility of the solutions. As Cohen and March point out in Chapter 10, if it is not possible to base organizational decisions on some perception of common goals and how they are to be achieved, then decisions will be taken in some other way. The ideal solution and problem may be happily united but this is not likely, especially in ambiguous organizations. Neither will decisions necessarily be consistent with one another because there is no common point of reference.

In such organizations decisions are more often taken by 'flight' or 'oversight'. Flight is a loose association of problems and solutions until such time as a more acceptable solution comes along. Oversight involves taking decisions without reference to other attendant problems. Thus the problem of placating parents whose children were in the final year of their education at the secondary modern school was 'resolved' by allowing those pupils to remain on the old site. This created serious organizational problems for Oakfields School and made the process of completing the amalgamation more difficult than it would otherwise have been.

Thus at Oakfields, many decisions were being made by both flight and oversight. The latter was the main process by which decisions were made about how to timetable the afternoon at the school. The major problem was how to create a timetable that would enable all subjects to be covered, allow space for pastoral work, and enable pupils and teachers to move from one room to another. Several solutions were adopted, including the teaching of additional periods during the official lunch break and combining registration with the pastoral period. However, these procedures were not popular among the teachers or pupils. The least popular decision was to abandon the idea of a form-based registration period after lunch. Instead, registration was to be carried out by whichever teacher taught the class in the first period in the afternoon. It was recognized from the outset that this was not an ideal solution and it soon became obvious to those trying to implement the system that it had fundamental flaws: neither did teachers know their classes well enough to carry out registration quickly and accurately, especially in the early days of the new school, nor did they know who should be present and who had good reason for being absent. The process of checking was cumbersome and follow-up could take a day or more. Teachers interviewed reported that they found great difficulty making the sytem work and that truancy, in the form of opting out from some lessons or missing afternoon school altogether, was rising. Some teachers, when under pressure to get their lessons started, simply forgot to do the register and attempted to complete it days later.

The head soon asked her staff to ensure that they carried out this process diligently. In an early Staff Bulletin (Monday, 7 October), she pointed out to those who taught fourth-formers, that a number of those pupils had gone missing from lessons after attending afternoon registration. However, this problem also occurred in the morning, because the same pupils were confident that afternoon registration would not be carried out in such a way as to detect their absence. Teachers wanted the process modified and made several suggestions, such as the use of an additional bell at the start of the afternoon to differentiate between registration and lessons. It was thought that this might act as a reminder to colleagues to take the register. The abandonment of form-based registration was therefore taken without due consideration of other problems, i.e. the difficulty of implementing it, the effect on pupil absences and the difficulty in checking. Why was it not remedied quickly?

In order to understand this it is necessary to see how solutions, problems, participants, issues and other choices interact. There were two main elements to this problem from the point of view of the headteacher and her senior management team. One was the extent to which colleagues were actually carrying out a process that had been devised by the senior management team and to which they were committed. They saw it as a question of their own competence as managers. The system was not ideal, but, in the view of the senior managers, especially in the early days of the autumn term, it was workable if it was implemented with goodwill by the staff. Evidence to the contrary tended to be discounted. Thus the solution to the registration problem had been created by and was owned by this group who were reluctant to respond to pressure for it to be changed, even though this pressure was based on strong evidence that it was not working. The senior management team discounted other related problems both before the decision was made and for some time after it was seen by others not to be working.

The headteacher found herself in a similar position. She wanted to be seen by her senior management team to be supporting them as part of her wider strategy of developing them into the type of team she wanted and needed. At the same time, the afternoon registration issue became closely associated with another, broader issue, that of how pupils should be controlled within the school. For the head, pupil control should be based on individual self-discipline. Others in the school had a more traditional, authoritarian or directive view of how children should be treated. Registration and attending classes was one of the battlegrounds upon which the issue of pupil control was fought. Could pupils be relied upon to attend classes even when they thought that insufficient checks were made on such attendance, or did they have to be coerced into being there? Thus, because other problems preceded the taking of this particular decision and because other issues became attached to it at a later stage, getting an inappropriate process changed took considerable time and energy on the part of more junior staff. The process was changed but not until the start of the second year when, it was argued, the ending of the split-site arrangement made this possible. In fact the split-site situation had very little bearing on the working of the process or upon timetabling problems that had preceded it.

If the registration issue was an example of problem solving by over-sight, the processes of staff appointment owed more to decision taking by flight. In this short chapter the extreme complexities of this process cannot be fully explored, especially at the crucial middle-management level where unions became involved and grievance procedures were initiated. At the senior management level the process was slightly less tendentious, although it began on an extremely controversial note.

One of the representatives of the LEA had very clear ideas about who should get each post based on her knowledge of two of the three schools. This inspector proposed that the headteacher-designate, as she was at that time, should not be involved in the appointment of her own senior management team on the grounds that she was party to giving information about a number of possible candidates. In the event, this proposal was not acted upon, partly because of strong representations from the Chairman of Governors of Oakfields School who was already taking part in the proceedings, although the head indicated in an interview that she was able to exert very little influence over the process of appointing her senior management team.

This proposal was the first indication that the process of staff appoint-ments was not to be one of resolution, i.e. fitting the most suitable, best qualified and most experienced people into the appropriate posts taking into account the expectations and opinions of the people most closely concerned with making the new school work. Applications for senior management posts were restricted to those members of staff in the three constituent schools on deputy head or senior teacher scales, and the number of posts to be filled was determined by the LEA's view about the appropriate number of senior staff for a school of this size. It was also made clear that as all staff were being appointed to new posts, there would be no opportunity for promotion. Because the amalgamation was, as much as anything, a cost-cutting exercise, rather than one based on clear educational goals, these constraints were understandable. Their effects, however, were to create severe problems for the management of the school in the long term.

The criteria for selecting the senior team are hard to identify. The existing post held seemed to be one major factor together with the avoidance of demotions as well as promotions. Seniority and experience counted for far less. The recommendations of the existing headteachers seemed to count for very little. In the event, even the decision to limit selection to those in senior posts in the three schools was not in the long-term interests of the new school, as there were a significant number of very capable staff just below senior teacher level who were more qualified than the group under consideration. Several of these teachers left Oakfields soon after it opened, thus leaving the school under-supported at a crucial level in its organization during a vital stage in its development.

The outcome of this process was to put together a team who were relatively strong on administration but who were not good at dealing with staff relationships or leading major curriculum initiatives. The least experienced of all the candidates became a deputy head while one of the more experienced people from the same constituent school was redesignated Senior Teacher in charge of Staff Development. This decision was difficult to understand in terms of the goals of the school because, as the head later commented, staff development ought to have been seen as the province of a deputy head. The senior management team, three deputies and two senior teachers, was also badly balanced in another respect. The three deputies were men and the two senior teachers were women. This presented an unfortunate role model for the girls in the newly formed school. Although the head was female, she was, by force of circumstance, less accessible to pupils than the members of the senior management team. The reaction of various teachers to the team has been touched upon above in another context but it was clear from interviews that this team, because it had not demonstrably been identified through a process of looking at what the school wanted to do and picking the most appropriate people to facilitate that endeavour, did not have the full confidence of the whole staff.

The creation of the senior management team had been seen as the solution to the problem of what to do with the existing senior staff rather than approached from the perspective of what kind of leadership was most needed by the school at that time. The head found herself presented with the problem of how to manage the school with the team that she had been given. Her solution was to take a far more active part in middle-management appointments, where she had more room for manoeuvre, and to create a strong tier of middle managers upon whom she came to depend heavily in the first year of the school's existence. This was, at best, a tactical position and was not that which she would have chosen in ideal circumstances.

At the end of the first term the head of Oakfields went into hospital and was away for most of the spring term. Many of the issues discussed here emerged in an even more intense form. Towards the end of the academic year the school was the subject of further rationalization plans that included the loss of its sixth form. It had no control over this decision. One of its senior deputy heads was seconded for 2 years to the nearby university and has since taken an advisor's job in another LEA. In March 1986, 5 years after her first appointment to the LEA, the head of Oakfields announced that she had been appointed to the headship of another school in a neighbouring LEA. This was a direct result of the proposals to remove the sixth form from the school.

It can be seen, therefore, that traditional models of school organization are not very useful in helping us to understand how and why a school like Oakfields is as it is. Traditional models of school organization, especially those developed by Corwin (1970), Lambert *et al.* (1970), Musgrove (1968) and Shipman (1968), attribute to schools characteristics such as clear goals, identifiable personnel, a relevant and explicit technology, and relationships based on positional rather than personal factors. These structural features are thought to produce consistency, predictability and stability. Taken together the extent to which a school's organization is thought to exhibit these characteristics indicates something about the nature of its authority and control structures. If an organization is found to be unpredictable or thought to be irrational in its decision making, then those who are subjected to this unpredictability or irrationality are aggrieved because such events are unexpected in the context of a formal organization. Similarly, when some sections of the school fail to respond to the demands of other sections in the expected way, a degree of tension is created between the sections and perhaps between the members of those sections. The expectations and the assumptions on which they are based may, however, rest on an unrealistic notion of the nature of schools as organizations.

In order to understand the responses of such schools as Oakfields to the situations in which they find themselves and over which they have little control, the traditional notion of the school as an hierarchical decision-making structure with a horizontal division into departments and a vertical division into authority levels needs to be abandoned. Such a conceptualiz-ation is unsuitable for the analysis of an organization attempting to cope with an unstable and unpredictable environment. Once it is recognized how decisions are taken in a situation of unclear technology, problematic goals and fluid membership, then the possibility is recognized of seeing patterns in the apparently unpredictable and disorderly process of making choices in an ambiguous organization. The fundamental importance of unclear technology, fluid membership and the problematic nature and position of educational goals has to be accorded due recognition in any analysis of the organization and management of a school such as Oakfields.

References

Bell, L. A. (1980). 'The School as an Organisation: A Reappraisal'. *British Journal of Sociology of Education*, **1**(2), 183–95.

Cohen, M. D. and March, J. G. (1974). *Leadership and Ambiguity: The American College President*. New York: McGraw-Hill.

Corwin, R. G. (1970). *Militant Professionalism. A Study of Organisational Conflicts in High Schools*. New York: Appleton-Century-Croft.

Lambert, R., Bullock, R. and Millham, S. (1970). *A Manual to the Sociology of the School*. London: Weidenfeld and Nicolson.

Musgrove, P. W. (1968). *The School as an Organisation*. London: Macmillan.

Shipman, M. D. (1968). *Sociology of the School*. London: Longman.

13

Management of higher education institutions in a period of contraction and uncertainty

John L. Davies and Anthony W. Morgan

[. . .]

Institutions of higher education as organizations

[. . .]As Richman and Farmer (1974) observe, 'top management, in the final analysis, is responsible for getting an adequate mesh between what the outside world wants, needs and expects from a given institution in terms of its goals, priorities and programmes, what the internal constituencies want, need and expect, and what the faculty is capable of delivering'. Scarce resources, coupled with the issue of goals, are at the heart of the problem of institutional decision making. It follows that the perceptions of the workings of the institution held by the various participants in decision making is a critical factor, especially whether those perceptions are normative, descriptive, explanatory or predictive.

There appear to be four main organizational models of the higher education institution. The *bureaucratic model* assumes that the institution comprises a formal organizational structure, with specified roles, clear hierarchies and chains of command, predetermined procedures and regulations. It is assumed that people behave and the organization works according to the formal structure (Weber, 1947). Richman and Farmer (1974) and Becher and Kogan (1980) observe that institutions are much less predictable than this prescription, because of the many social, psychological and self-actualization needs unfulfilled in the model; the increasing number of issues which have no precedent and venture solution; and the fact that the head does not exercise unequivocal managerial authority.

The *collegial model* (Millett, 1962) assumes a fraternity of scholars seeking individual and collective fulfilment, through full participation in decision making. In this model, consensus decision making by academics does not admit of an influential administrative role. The model does tend to ignore the existence of academic hierarchy and academic ritual, and assumes, often wrongly, a genuine spirit of cooperation, deep commitment to the institution, similar shared values and abundant resources.

The *political model* (Baldridge, 1971a, b) takes conflict as the natural state of academic affairs, and focuses on the issues created by interest groups with different goals, values, styles of operation and methods of generating and pursuing policy preferences. Participation is fluid, decisions are normally negotiated compromises, achieved informally and processed through legitimate decision-making arenas which translate pressures into policy. While a helpful explanation of current phenomena, it clearly does not apply to all institutional conditions.

The *organized anarchy model* (Cohen and March, 1974; Olsen and March, 1974) posed the problem of the institution being caught in an 'anarchy trap' as a result of ambiguous goals, ambiguous means–ends relationships, ambiguous systems of rewards and sanctions, high autonomy of subordinates with strong extra-institutional affiliations, and weak market feedback mechanisms. Decentralization is necessary because leaders and administrators are not sufficiently knowledgeable in all disciplines to be able to make informed decisions (Corson, 1973; Parsons and Platt, 1973). Cohen and March (1974) believe that decision processes in institutions are not so much mechanisms for solving problems, but more for participants to air grievances and pose preferences which may have but passing relevance to the issue ostensibly under discussion. Their conclusion is that the institution head needs to develop tactical responses in order to influence decisions. Unlike Enderud (1977), Cohen and March are not so much interested in strategic policy generation – a significant limitation – and somewhat underplay the extent to which institutions can be managed.

None of these types, of course, are pure forms. Becher and Kogan (1980) indicate the linkages which occur because of the functioning of individual managers such as vice-chancellors, directors, registrars, deans and heads of department. They operate both within the hierarchy and the collegium, through executive offices, committees and informal political arenas. Richman and Farmer (1974) develop a more comprehensive open systems approach, with a view to prescription and prediction, coupled with a strong contingency element. Enderud (1977) locates the four models outlined above in a phased evolution of policy decisions, where each has a role to play at a particular time in the delivery of effective policy. However, the incidence of contraction inevitably generates more insecurity and thus more conflict and politicization than in times of plenty or even steady state. In general, therefore, the political and organized anarchy models seem to have more affinity with the current situation in higher education.

The contemporary external pressures for institutions to develop corporate policies for the internal management of programmes, personnel, finance and space are clearly very considerable. We therefore have widespread plans for senior management to develop rational and imaginative policies which are academically sound, financially viable and politically acceptable, both internally and externally. In this case, many highly intelligent institutional heads would tend to adopt systematic approaches of generating policy; these incorporate a definition of desired outcomes, the identification and weighing of alternative solutions and options, the attribution of costs and benefits, a decision based on a mix of appropriate options, and a systematic evaluation of efficiency and effectiveness of the adopted policy mixes. Each of these activities is impregnated with potential conflict and disagreement, which clearly hinders satisfactory progress. We observed the following tendencies in the institutions we studied:

- joint policy decisions are slow and problematic to make;
- decisions which are carried through are usually partial, short range and based on compromise;
- policy decisions and criteria have to be attacked over and over again before a conventional wisdom gets established;
- more institutional bureaucracy is created, in the sense of more participant involvement, more requests for information to executives, more referrals of decision for sub-committee consideration, etc.;
- the academic finds himself in several concurrent dilemmas: he does not like meetings yet he must generate or attend them to preserve his interests and influence, the direction and substance of his plans; he does not wish to spend too much time himself on planning matters, yet he is reluctant to trust others, including administrators; he wishes to plan in the sense of having a stable framework in which to operate, yet he resents being constrained by a substantive plan; he wants a power fixer on whom he can rely to sort out difficult issues, yet he resents the growth of power centres which are beyond the effective control of himself and his colleagues;
- policy decisions, given the economic realities, environmental uncertainties and political context, may increasingly be concerned with the marginal decision consistent with a very broad loose framework rather than the grand fixed strategy of a development plan. Point of specificity in planning may be possible on particular issues, but this in itself does not remove the anarchy trap;
- difficulties with planning and policy making originate with questions of reluctance and inability of participants to plan, namely to imagine the future of the institution as a whole. The role of the rector or central planner would thus seem to be as much concerned with creating an appropriate psychological climate in which participants can be creative, as with the more conventional technical aspects of information collection and analysis.

In this context, yearnings for corporate rationality may be illusory.

It becomes quite vital, therefore, for institutional leaders charged with the development of policy to have a very precise understanding of how their institutions behave or are likely to behave. If they assume collegiality where none exists and push decisions accordingly, they will very likely be disappointed. Both the policy-making process they develop, and the roles in policy formation which they play, need to be carefully attuned to the variables of the particular situation.

[. . .]

The political nature of change in institutions of higher education

All kinds of power problems are implied in the discussion so far. Decision-making and change processes are basically reflective of the underlying power structure and the environmental context of institutions (Clark, 1978). Institutions of higher education are built around a strong core of professionals who exercise considerable autonomy and influence over central institutional processes. Decision-making and change processes are therefore characterized by a substantial degree of bargaining, persuasion and manoeuvring, hence 'gamesmanship' or politics, among peers. Were educational and research outputs and 'production functions' more clearly understood and quantifiable, the degree of gamesmanship would be reduced although certainly not eliminated. But because decision making in institutions of higher education is characterized by a wide distribution of power among numerous, semi-independent entities and by what has been described as the 'complexity of joint action' (Pressman and Wildavsky, 1973), any constructive change moving through the organization is subject to such 'political' forces as:

> the players involved; what they regard as the stakes; their strategies and tactics; their resources for playing; the rules of play (which stipulate the conditions for winning); the rules of 'fair' play (boundaries of acceptable play); nature of communications among players; and the degree of uncertainty surrounding the outcomes (Bardach, 1978).

Institutional leaders have always had to contend with such forces, but the prevailing consensus or collegial norms, coupled with a certain respect for the authority of legitimate office-holders, was usually sufficient to sort out behavioural aberrations without too much fuss. Under conditions of expansion, the conflicting interests of organizational sub-groups could most often be accommodated by giving partial funding now and the promise of future funds later. As long as powerful individuals and groups received what they perceived to be reasonable shares of expanding resources, the core organizational coalitions were maintained in relative harmony (Cyert and March, 1963). Those not receiving their fair share and who had marketability elsewhere often exercised that ultimate market sanction against deterioration in organizational performance – 'exit' (Hirschman, 1970).

The politics of institutional change under conditions of instability or contraction are different from those most commonly characteristic of expanding organizations in that they are more intense and 'defensive'. As resources to meet the policy commitments and funding demands of competing organizational groups have diminished, institutional administrators have experienced an increased level of conflict, particularly as options to exit the organization have diminished, leaving what Hirschman (1970) terms 'voice' or the political response, as the only viable option for most members of the organization. In their study of 42 American institutions, Cohen and March (1974) confirm that financial adversity did result in a precipitous rise in conflict and in the time required to arrive at decisions. Richman and Farmer (1974) and Baldridge (1971a) observe that in many cases, none of the formal or informal ordinary mechanisms of power can cope. Non-compliance and the limited effect of traditional sanctions lead to increasing reliance on regulations, due process and sterile legalism.

[. . .]

The process of generating effective policy

Alternative views of policy formation

So far it has been argued that there are many mutually reinforcing factors within and without the contemporary higher education institution, which place severe limits on the extent to which it can be managed with any degree of certainty. Yet the situation imperatives are invariably for clear, firm guidelines as soon as possible to allay fears and solve problems. So what avenues are open to senior management to develop effective policies to cope with contraction and its attendant issues? At a conceptual level, Enderud (1977) postulates three possible courses of action:

1 To straighten out the ambiguities by increasing the degree of rationality and structure in decision making. This may involve:

- increasing the degree of structure and formality in organizational charts, regulations and procedures related to planning (highly unlikely to succeed, as non-compliance and informal bypassing of formal structures are likely to increase; as a result, information overload will create reactions against more clarification);
- increasing coercion by the hierarchy (unlikely to succeed, given the increasing democratization of institutions and the shortage of sanctions to enforce the coercion);
- applying radical shocks to the system, through controlling key elements which influence academics' job satisfaction – validation, monitoring and evaluation of research; control of monies; manipulating balance of teaching, research and administration time (possible, but requires the

existence of a steady state or contraction, and a stable coalition of appropriately strong institutional interest groups, to make it last);
- actively seeking to manipulate and control all the variables which go to create the ambiguities. If these factors are responsible for creating the bulk of our planning difficulties in the first place, it would appear to be logical to try to remove them, if they hinder the effectiveness of the institution. (This would seem to be well beyond the reasonable capabilities of institutional administrations.)

2 To accept the ambiguities of the situation as inevitable, and use a 'muddling-through' style of planning process – non-interventionist and procedural. If this course is followed, it may rest on the assumption that it is highly desirable to maintain the ambiguity in order consciously to limit the influence of macro-policy matters, and to protect the essential characteristics of academic autonomy. It is a matter of judgement whether external agencies would enable this stance to be taken, what the costs to the institution would be, and whether the problems associated with the contraction would ever be resolved.

3 To evolve a policy/planning process which recognizes the existence of ambiguities at certain points, but uses them positively and consciously to arrive at workable decisions. This would seem to require a fusion of the explicit elements of Lindblom's theory of muddling through, and Enderud's (1977) four-phase model. The assumptions would seem to be that:

- any planning system which attempts to create a massive and fundamental rethink and recasting of the nature of the institution and a considerable switching of resources across the board over a short time-scale is most unlikely to succeed. A planning system which encourages and facilitates shifts at the margin on a continuing and incremental basis is likely to succeed;
- the opportunity must be seized within the planning process to ensure that relatively small-scale changes have maximum pay-off in psychological impact and practical effect, particularly to undermine historical relics and create precedents;
- such successful planning decisions will need to create internal commitment to the means of achieving an end, without necessarily having widespread agreement to the end itself, which is likely to be the subject of value differences;
- successful planning decisions may be more opportunist than cyclical in their timing and incidence. They may not necessarily coincide with particular stages in the budget process, but do not have to be *ad hoc* or unco-ordinated in intent as a result of this;
- such a planning process may call for more political/behavioural skills than technical skills (enhanced sensitivities to the realities of others' beliefs, preferences and modes of action);

- a firm and stable coalition needs to exist over the period of the genesis and implementation of the decision, consisting of key groups of people who, to collaborate, need incentives, which may be provided by the administration. Furthermore, they must be determined to use the formal structure to effect their desired changes, but in ways best suited to their particular purpose.

A model of policy formation for conditions of politicization and ambiguity

Figure 13.1 is an extension by Davies (1980) of Enderud's four-phase model of policy formation. Policy here is concerned with the non-routine, non-programmed decisions of high visibility and potential conflict. The essence of the model lies in the following:

1 The sequence is based on a gradual evolution of the planning decision, to ensure that there is a proper allowance for an essentially high ambiguous period (phase 1); a political period (phase 2); a collegial period (phase 3); and an implementation/executive period (phase 4). To miss any phase, or to allow insufficient time for it, is to invite problems subsequently, because one may find that, for example, the wrong participants have been coupled (phase 1), or that one comes to phase 4 without having tested a key group's support of the proposition. Jumping over one phase may well create the necessity of a loopback; thus, if one is in phase 4, which is clearly not working, a return to phase 1 may be necessary to redefine the problem, or to phase 2 to build a workable coalition of interests, or to phase 3 to use additional validation criteria in respect of the proposal. The loopback may be a decision of the sensitive vice-chancellor who realizes the necessary foundations have not been laid; on the other hand (and less desirably!), it may be forced on him by hostile groups who are just not happy with having a possibly ill-conceived and partially tested decision thrust upon them.

2 While one may have a specific planning strategy in mind to cope with a series of problems, one does not start by exposing this in its fullest glories! On the contrary, the starting point is a close definition of the dimensions of the problem to which one's plan is related in terms which (a) appeal to people from various positions on the power spectrum and (b) are internally consistent with any preferred solution one may have. The administrator then has the considerable advantage of being in the business of identifying problems rather than indiscriminately peddling bright ideas which may be perceived as irrelevant or threatening. Planning in this context thus has a very strong element of problem diagnosis.

3 The university head has a significant role of creating communication links and dialogues between parties who may have the capability of developing perspectives on a planning problem. They may be part of some formal structure or key members of an informal group which nevertheless has

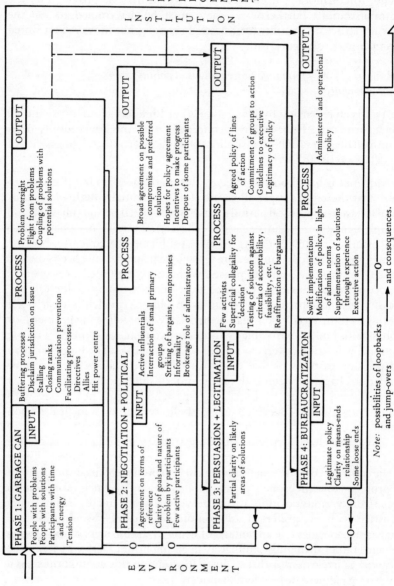

Figure 13.1 A four-phase political systems model of policy formation (after Enderud, 1977).

something positive to offer. At its most sophisticated, the vice-chancellor's or administrator's role involves coalition building between potentially like-minded groups.

4 The administrator will soon recognize that there are many arenas in which to act in any of the four phases. Enderud indeed makes the point that the formal phase 3, which gives ostensible legitimacy to the planning proposal or document, is likely to be the emptiest in terms of real argument and contribution. Other avenues are likely to be informal (the bar, the common room, the golf club) – ones which are appropriate to the needs of the particular phase concerned; ones which make most sense to the participants one is trying to involve; and ones which take the pressure off the administrator. Those left holding the baby of a particular problem or specific solution are easily turned on or deserted when hard choices are needed. Using the four-phase processes to share the ownership of a problem or solution with others, therefore, is important.

5 The plan or proposal itself has the opportunity of evolving through the phases not only as an increasingly complex and detailed guide to subsequent action, but as an increasingly acceptable political, educational and resource package. Consequently, the model is one which facilitates close attention to task and process concurrently – one of the perpetual problems of organizational theorists and practitioners (Blake *et al.*, 1981).

Applications of the model

When the model shown in Fig. 13.1 is applied to the British cases studied by the authors, some very interesting perspectives begin to emerge. The tentative conclusions (at the time of writing) are:

1 There are few cases where agreed policy requiring contraction has been delivered at the end of phase 3 in order to be implemented at phase 4. Senates or academic boards have very often referred back executive proposals for departmental rationalization encompassed in a 'grand strategy' type of document, thus creating a loopback, usually to phase 1, for a redefinition of the problem.

2 The reasons why proposals have foundered eventually at phase 3 are normally to be found in the neglect or failure of critical processes in the preceding phases 1 and 2, for example:

- failure to appreciate the magnitude and dynamics of political feeling generated by proposals;
- neglect of informal action by senior administrators (especially phases 1 and 2) and an undue reliance on the ability of senates to process controversial proposals;
- reluctance of top management to get involved in bargains and incentives to develop support for policy packages (phases 2 and 3);
- unwillingness of top management to play a brokerage function between

interest groups, particularly in the passage of vital information (phases 1 and 2);
- neglect of the vital function of building alliances in support of proposals, even when potential opposition groups had not yet crystallized their joint preferences, and were still disorganized.

3 In all cases, the head of the institution staked his personal reputation as chairman of a steering committee/working party/development committee, to produce strategies for contraction, thus jeopardizing his subsequent freedom of manoeuvre, especially in full senate meetings.

4 The working party concept, while a time-honoured device of collegial contemplation, has tended in places to act as a closed system collecting 'objective' information and presenting it cold to senates without prior political preparations.

5 Grand strategy documents give the distinct impression of being ultimate statements, rather than snapshots on the way to an evolving solution. Consequently, in full senate debates, they tend to polarize positions into 'winners' and 'losers': in general, this is not a good strategy for managing change.

6 The grand strategy mode of operation is clearly very vulnerable, especially when all the critical information on the performance of departments underlying such analyses is not made publicly available. This is usually for admirably civilized reasons of not wishing to expose too cruelly the weaknesses of colleagues' departmental leadership. Senates have interesting ways of reacting to disturbing tidings, not the least being the almost intuitive formation of negative coalitions – the collegium defending itself against the bureaucracy!

7 Some institutions which have undergone the harrowing experience of having policies defeated have learned a great deal about the process of managing change; there is considerable evidence that some of the tactics used once will not be used again – or will be substantially modified.
[. . .]

References

Baldridge, J. V. (1971a). *Power and Conflict in the University*. New York, Wiley.
Baldridge, J. V. (1971b). *Academic Governance*. Berkeley, Calif., McCutchan.
Bardach, E. (1978). *The Implementation Game*. Cambridge, Mass., Institute of Technology.
Becher, T. and Kogan, M. (1980). *Process and Structure in Higher Education*. London, Heinemann.
Blake, R., Mouton, J. S. and Williams, M. S. (1981). *The Academic Administrator Grid*. San Francisco, Jossey-Bass.
Clark, B. R. (1978). 'Academic power: Concepts, modes and perspectives'. *In* Van de Graaff, J. H. *et al.* (eds), *Academic Power*. New York, Praeger.

Cohen, M. and March, J. G. (1974). *Leadership and Ambiguity*. New York, McGraw-Hill.

Corson, J. J. (1973). 'Perspectives on the university compared with other organizations'. *In* Perkins, J. A. (ed.), *The University as an Organisation*. New York, McGraw-Hill, pp. 156–69.

Cyert, R. M. and March, J. G. (1963). *A Behavioural Theory of the Firm*. Englewood Cliffs, N.J., Prentice Hall.

Davies, J. L. (1980). 'The role of the university rector in policy formation in the contemporary context of steady state and uncertainty'. *CRE New Series*, **51**, hind quarter.

Enderud, H. G. (1977). *Four Faces of Leadership in the Academic Organisation*. Copenhagen, Nyt. Nordisk Forlag.

Hirschman, A. O. (1970). *Exit, Voice and Loyalty Responses to Decline in Firms, Organizations, and States*. Cambridge, Mass., Harvard University Press.

Millett, J. (1962). *The Academic Community*. New York, McGraw-Hill.

Mingle, J. C. (1981). *The Challenge of Retrenchment*. San Francisco, Jossey-Bass.

Olsen, J. P. and March, J. G. (1974). *Ambiguity and Choice in Organisations*. Bergen Universitetsforlaget.

Parsons, T. and Platt, G. M. (1973). *The American University*. Cambridge, Mass., Harvard University Press.

Pressman, J. L. and Wildavsky, A. (1973). *Implementation*. Berkeley, University of California Press.

Richman, B. M. and Farmer, R. N. (1974). *Leadership, Goals and Power in Higher Education*. San Francisco, Jossey-Bass.

Weber, M. (1947). *The Theory of Social and Economic Organisation*. New York, Free Press.

Author index

Subject index